Winging It

Winging It

Dispatches from an (Almost) Empty Nest

Catherine Goldhammer

HUDSON
STREET
PRESS

HUDSON STREET PRESS

Published by the Penguin Group

Penguin Group (USA) Inc., 375 Hudson Street, New York, New York 10014, U.S.A. • Penguin Group (Canada), 90 Eglinton Avenue East, Suite 700, Toronto, Ontario, Canada M4P 2Y3 (a division of Pearson Penguin Canada Inc.) • Penguin Books Ltd., 80 Strand, London WC2R 0RL, England • Penguin Ireland, 25 St. Stephen's Green, Dublin 2, Ireland (a division of Penguin Books Ltd.) • Penguin Group (Australia), 250 Camberwell Road, Camberwell, Victoria 3124, Australia (a division of Pearson Australia Group Pty. Ltd.) • Penguin Books India Pvt. Ltd., 11 Community Centre, Panchsheel Park, New Delhi – 110 017, India • Penguin Group (NZ), 67 Apollo Drive, Rosedale, North Shore 0632, New Zealand (a division of Pearson New Zealand Ltd.) • Penguin Books (South Africa) (Pty.) Ltd., 24 Sturdee Avenue, Rosebank, Johannesburg 2196, South Africa

Penguin Books Ltd., Registered Offices: 80 Strand, London WC2R 0RL, England

First published by Hudson Street Press, a member of Penguin Group (USA) Inc.

First Printing, October 2008
10   9   8   7   6   5   4   3   2   1

REGISTERED TRADEMARK—MARCA REGISTRADA
HUDSON
STREET
PRESS

CIP data is available.
ISBN 978-1-59463-048-4

Printed in the United States of America
Set in Perpetua and Wendy

PUBLISHER'S NOTE
All names and identifying characteristics have been changed to protect the privacy of the individuals involved.

This book is printed on acid-free paper.

For Henry

Contents

Introduction

When my daughter was twelve, we moved from the affluent suburb of her childhood to a tiny fixer-upper in a run-down seaside town in New England. I was newly divorced, and she was newly a teenager. We got chickens and we moved (in that order) and we renovated the new little house. I wrote a book, and my daughter grew from an eccentric gangly girl into a deep and mysterious young woman. I wondered, at some point in those days, when life changes were coming in waves, one quickly following another in massive seismic shifts—the year of the divorce and the year of the move and the year of the book—what the next "year" would be. I should have seen it coming, but I did not.

Some kids are moving from the moment of birth. At the park toddlers blithely walk down slides or off the edges of wooden forts, and then climb back up to do it all again. Not mine. Harper wasn't a climber or a jumper or a runner. She watched, and talked, and drew. She drew three hundred pictures of ballerinas in the course of a week's vacation when she was three. I then stopped buying pads of paper and instead bought rolls of shelf paper, which she covered, edge to edge, with elaborate universes of tiny stick figure girls. I built her complicated forts made out of couch cushions, bamboo poles, and long pieces of sea green silk. She never played in them. It drove me crazy. Years later I mentioned it.

"Oh," she said, "I thought you knew. I didn't want to *play* in them. I wanted to see how you *built* them."

I quickly learned that the primary joy and challenge of parenthood was to trust the spirit I had given birth to, and to know when to rein in and when to let go. Harper was simultaneously a homebody and a mental rover. She didn't sleep through the night until she was ten, complaining of "the mist" that pervaded her room in the middle of the night. (I believed in the mist, but had never seen it.) She didn't like to be away from home, and three-day elementary school trips required me to write two notes a day, seal them, and secret them in her duffle. She stopped reading them long before I stopped writing them.

Of course, the trips away became longer and I got more and more used to them, and so did she, until time away was just another part of life. She was always ready for the next step before I was and when she left for a college program in philosophy the summer she was fifteen, she, of course, did fine.

And so did I, mostly. Just one lost weekend and a few weekdays given to wandering around clueless. But then I got into the swing of things. I got up at the same time every day and fed Sam, the red hound, Monkey, the ghost gray cat, and the chickens. I had breakfast by the window. I did worthwhile things: made phone calls, moved my office from the tiny (and muddy) mudroom to my daughter's old bedroom on the first floor (she had fled to the attic), and painted its bookcases a glossy black. I had a certain kind of energy that comes with time and the ability to concentrate. I got a lot done. I felt virtuous and productive. I made a Web site. I mailed the publication announcements for my first book. I had that reaching-out sort of feeling. The *anything could happen now* feeling. I was vital. I was on the upswing.

But every time my cell phone buzzed with a text message from Harper, I leaped. I became somewhat adept at "texting" back. Though the verb offended my sensibilities, the form of communication beat the sealed notes. Even so, it took me a half hour to send a reasonably amusing message. I went to the phone store and pondered the BlackBerry and the Treo. Perhaps I needed one of those, I reasoned. After all, they had a full keyboard and Internet connectivity, and the BlackBerry in particular struck me as a writerly, busy thing to have. This was not a new preoccupation. I fairly often tried to talk myself into getting a BlackBerry. As if having one would spice up my life. How, I did not know.

Then, in the back-and-forth of text messages and separate days, I began to understand what the next seismic shift was going to be. You have your children and you can't possibly imagine that one day they will walk off toward their own horizon. You really can't. You know it, but you don't. And then it happens and you have to let them go. It wasn't that I didn't know this. Not to get all Kahlil Gibran about it, but our children really *are* the arrows we send out into the future, and I knew that my daughter was walking toward that moment with intent, and that she was way ahead of me in readiness. According to my friends who'd been there before me, knowing it didn't necessarily help.

"We pour everything into them," an uncommonly gentle friend said with uncharacteristically bitter humor. "And then they leave us, the little bastards."

And so, after years and years—of scraping oatmeal off the floor with a spatula, retrieving plastic octopi from the mouths of toddlers, navigating the shoals of kindergarten and friendships and boyfriends, learner's permits, driver's licenses, the specters of sex, drugs, and alcohol, the mind-opening bands with their strange names and poetic lyrics, the brain-sucking nightmare of MySpace and Facebook, the iPod with its thousands of songs, the singing lessons, the art classes, the heart-stopping riding lessons with their massive horses and five-foot jumps, the ambitions, the passions, the existential angst, the opportunity to revisit the Glass family, Rilke, and *Zen and the Art of Motorcycle Maintenance*—you finally see it on the horizon. There you are. You. About to be returned to yourself.

Part One

These Windswept and Rocky Shores

Washed Up

Harper came back from the philosophy program with an Italian boyfriend and the announcement that she wasn't going back to high school. The Italian boyfriend, a dark-haired, model-handsome, gangly, joyous boy, full of faith and old-fashioned chivalry, was a surprise. The declaration was not. Harper hated high school. She had chafed against the confines of formal education and had longed for something more, the mental equivalent of *death-defying*. It hadn't come as a surprise when, instead of attending a cushy art camp in a bucolic setting, she went instead to the academically rigorous philosophy camp at a Catholic college with dorm rooms full of battered wooden castoffs and screens that only marginally fit the windows.

"I want a true educational experience," she'd said. And so, although she was not a Catholic, or religious at all for that matter, off she'd gone, along with three suitcases full of stylish clothes and seven pairs of shoes. She called only a few times, and sent me text messages sporadically. Her

language was different. When she used the words *pure* and
religious crisis in the same text message, I, fearing she was
under pressure from the Catholic majority, freaked out.
"Mom," she wrote, "I brought my intelligence here, too."

They read hundreds of pages a night. They read Plato
and Aristotle and studied the significance of the death of
Socrates. They wrote papers on *the meaning of melancholy*
and *the place of the poet in society* and *the meaning of courage.*
And then she came back knowing something about the
depth and breadth of her future. I knew within minutes of
seeing her something I had known before but not really
believed. She was going to grow up and do her job. She
was going to leave me. She would set out on the journey
of her life, and I would watch her go.

Then something new happened to me, something that
had never happened before in my life as a mother. I was
overcome with envy. Envy of the new life she was bound
for, envy of the education she would receive, envy of the
way she wore her clothes, her pale skin, her Italian boyfriend. For a deep bell of truth had been rung inside her.
And I wondered, with what I hoped was wry self-pity, if
that bell would ever again ring for me. Worse, what if it
never *had* rung? What if I had lived a bell-less life? I felt
used up, washed up, washed out, and over the hill. Not to
mention wildly—if pessimistically—overdramatic. I was
jaded and unhopeful. My life was over. I was fifty-five.

❧

Even I could see that it was a bit too soon for life to be over. But things were no longer interesting. I knew too much, about everything, it appeared, to be excited about anything ever again, about learning or men or the future. Even books failed me. A year like the one in which I read Norman Rush's *Mating*, A. S. Byatt's *Possession*, Jane Smiley's *Ordinary Love and Good Will*, and Elizabeth Von Arnim's *The Enchanted April* would never come again, I was sure. Not in a million years. And certainly not in whatever number of years were left to me.

I wondered how many miserable, washed-up, bad-book years that might be. My neighbor Phoebe—a cheerful and unpredictable soul who I once saw dancing on her roof—told me about a Web site on which one can take a test to determine one's expected longevity. I figured I would never take that test because I was worried, even though my life was over, that it actually *was* over, and I figured I could live without that knowledge in the brief time that remained to me. But curiosity got the best of me, and I logged on, took the questionnaire, and, with a combination of trepidation and morbid disregard, clicked the "compute" button.

Ninety-three. I would live until I was ninety-three years old. Longer if I exercised more and lost a few pounds.

I had almost forty years left. Maybe thirty years before things started to go south. Thirty years was the amount of time I had lived since I was twenty-five. I was awfully young when I was twenty-five, and when I compared myself then with myself now, in many ways I was barely the same person.

Being washed up is one thing when you are living blithely in the paltry quality of one day at a time. It is another thing entirely when you think of thirty years of paltry quality. My father used to say, "People say that life is too short. But it isn't. It's *long*." A friend of mine took the longevity quiz and told her sister that they could expect to live to 103. No response from her sister.

"However, if you are a smoker, you can subtract eight years."

"I'm taking up smoking today," said her sister.

In the days following Harper's return, I noticed that the other things that had once filled my nest were also dwindling. My six chickens (with which I had bribed Harper when, at twelve, she refused to move from our predivorce house to the cottage we now inhabited) had dwindled to two. Dead chickens, though still sad on an individual level, had also become a depressing proof of existential failure. My first book was off in the world on its own. The tour was over. Gone were the heady days of editing and proof-reading, phone calls from agents, publishers' e-mails, and trips to New York, where the halls of the Penguin building had seemed *hallowed*.

I didn't think I was depressed, exactly. I got up every morning and took my walk on the seawall. I watched the guy surfing the length of Six Mile Beach tied to a giant kite. I watched the tall laconic gentleman followed by three tiny jingling Yorkshire terriers, the Asian woman who had dyed the ears of her tiny white poodle blue, and the young man playing a mournful accordion while two large Labradors ran in perfect tandem, step matching step, bound matching bound, into the ocean and back out again, turning and turning again like wild black horses.

The seawall reminded me, every time I walked it, why I lived in Six Mile Beach. Every season brought a different kind of beauty. In the fall and winter great northeasters broke over the houses across the salt pond on which I lived and the wind rocked the walls of my small house. In the spring, the fleets of boats, with their lobster pots or choruses of clanking halyards, returned to the waters. In the summer, flocks of swans and egrets and herons flew overhead, the mockingbird took up residence in the apple tree, and my neighbors approached their gardens with determination. I was proud of the town, of its beauty and its quirky citizens. For this and other reasons, I got up every day and life seemed good. Then I'd realize how desperately in *need* of a life I was, because sooner or later in the day, usually sooner, I would be overcome by an unruly interest in Italy.

I had become obsessed not with the Italian boyfriend, though I thought he was very cool, but with the *idea* of an Italian boyfriend, the life I might lead if I indeed *had* an Italian boyfriend, though clearly that was not going to happen since everything in my life was now useless and nothing that interesting was ever going to happen to me again. That did not dim my curiosity. What were the houses like in Italy? What was the climate? Were people in Milan more stylish than people in Rome? Did Italians have as many pets as we do or dye their dog's ears blue? In northern Italy, near the Alps, were the stars brighter? Was Tuscany really all it was cracked up to be?

And it wasn't just idle wondering. I did research. I googled houses in Italy. They are not made of wood. Stone is very popular, and brick. Everything looks as though it has been hewn from the millennia. I checked the prices of these houses. I wasn't too sure about euro conversion, but those houses were clearly a lot cheaper than houses on the coast of New England. If my daughter married the good Italian boy and ended up living in Italy, which I was pretty sure she should, she would live in a village north of Milan, be an artist, and have two children, both boys, possibly twins. She would speak Italian. She would be elegant and beautiful and *European*. I would sell my cottage then and move to Italy, into one of those stone houses. Or I would divide my time between Italy and the coast of New England. All I had to do was marry my fifteen-year-old agnostic daughter to a conservative seventeen-year-old Italian Catholic. I was in relatively deep trouble, thoughtwise. I knew that.

I discovered that I was a font of unwanted relationship wisdom. I knew just about everything, it turned out, and was not afraid to offer my counsel whenever my daughter asked, and even when she didn't. And mostly she didn't. She really did *not* want to know. I asked too many questions about the Italian, and she was getting irritated. I wanted to know what town he lived in and when school started. I wanted to know as much as possible, since she was going to marry him, though I didn't tell *her* that. I bought her an Italian-English dictionary and got a book of Italian sayings from the library. She put them both on the hall table for rapid return.

"You don't want these?" I asked.

"Not really," she said.

Are you *crazy*? I thought.

Harper's friend Rose had attended the same summer program and was also in love with an Italian boy. At first she and Harper wept a lot, and pined. Then there was a winsome, enchanted stage in which long bouts of instant messaging took place and everyone knew exactly what time it was in Italy. Common sense did battle with romance. They would go to Italy next summer. Love would conquer all. They wouldn't go. Nothing would happen. I was on the side of love conquering all. I don't know why. I knew it didn't. But I wanted it to, for her.

"I am your suffering boy," wrote the Italian boy. "You are the boss of the magical sadness of this man." He sent her a mix CD he'd labeled "Devastation," which we played in the car. It was full of Bruce Springsteen and U2 songs.

"He likes anthems," I hypothesized.

"He likes big ideas," my daughter said.

"What do you mean?" I asked.

"I don't know," she said. "He likes the *sun*." I sighed.

I knew I had to stop when she accused me. "You'd be mad at me if I decided I didn't like him, wouldn't you," she said. It was not a question, and I didn't have to think long. She was right. I wanted her to settle her romantic future now so I wouldn't have to worry. She should choose this boy, whose idea of a really good time was hunting truffles and running from wild boars in the Swiss Alps. He was a good boy, smart and loyal, and rooted in the land of the ages.

She was a little bit worn out by it, and by the language barrier.

"The fact that he doesn't speak English is becoming difficult."

I can order you a really good Italian language program, I thought. I only thought it. I was learning. But the voice in my head insisted, *It doesn't get any better than that! Go for it! Just wait several more years,* I thought, *and then you can marry him. It isn't that long.*

I held on to the phrase book.

Like a Fish

One of my only distractions from Italy was the mail. I was discovering that one of the things about writing a book, it turns out, is that you get a lot of mail. I don't know why, but you do. And in this life there is very little that is as good as mail. No one gets much of it these days. Even before the advent of e-mail, the letter was dying a slow death. There were times in my youth when heavy envelopes crossed my doorway frequently, pages and pages of scrawled handwriting, full of philosophy and poems and mad, passionate ideas. Those days had gone by, but I had nostalgia for them. Once I had been thrown into a fit of envy by a neighbor, a middle-aged poet who had recently had a book published by a classy little press. He was a humble fellow and when he talked about his book he laid one hand over his heart as if he were going to weep or pass out. And as if to prove my as yet unformulated theory about book publication and mail, this guy had the most amazing mail. He got so much mail that he had to hang a large canvas bag on his doorknob to handle the overflow. I could see the bag from my office and it was always full. Always. It made me want to spit.

Now, since my own book had been published, I got manuscripts and cards and books and letters and announcements and postcards and more letters. I carried them around with me, or used them as bookmarks. I liked to read them more than once and I never threw any of them away. Every time a piece of mail arrived, I marveled. I laid it on the kitchen table unopened and looked at it for a while as if it were capable of great things.

I got letters from family, strangers, and long-lost friends. When my book came out, I'd had some announcements made and had sent them out to people I didn't talk to very much, my Christmas card list, old classmates from high school and college and graduate school, and, in a fit of God knows what kind of insanity, to a bunch of old boyfriends whom I'd googled out of obscurity. And a number of days after sending my announcements into the world like little waves of hands, I opened my mailbox and found a letter from Hunter.

I'd met Hunter in graduate school. He was a painter. I was a poet. The poets and the painters usually did not consort. I consorted with both poets and painters and with a history major with a gap-toothed smile and coffee-colored skin. With Hunter I'd had not one, but two (count them!) unsuccessful relationships and, in between being dumped the first time and being dumped the second time, a long best-friendship. *Years* long. Then there was that second dumping, which included infidelity on his part and a lot of weeping on both of our parts, his writing me letters that I returned, and my finally telling him that I never wanted to see or hear from him again. How this history had translated into my sending him a book announcement, I didn't know.

The first letter from Hunter was sweet. He asked me to forgive him. Part of the letter was typed and part handwritten. I liked seeing his handwriting again. I liked remembering what it looked like and thinking of other, pre-broken-heart letters and packages written and addressed in that handwriting. I remembered why I had loved him. I had a little bit of a fantasy then that we would become friends again, or maybe even have a romance, one of those met-again-after-twenty-years-and-lived-happily-ever-after stories. Never mind that I believed that people really didn't change; maybe he *had* changed. He would be devoted. I conjured up images of a vacation I took every year with a large number of very old friends in a worse-than-rustic place on miles of marshes near the ocean. I imagined that he would come to see me in that place and that all of my friends would see us together and think, *Oh, see how much he loves her.*

So I had that fantasy about Hunter and in it we became the couple you might see at the country fair walking to the oxen pull, the interesting, smart-looking pair you would notice and wonder about. I'm not sure what I thought. Maybe that the two breakups were, I don't know, *mistakes.* Phoebe was, I must say, extremely excited about the letter. We sat at the big round table on my deck, under the scalloped white canopy. A small breeze ruffled its edges.

"Oh, my *God!*" she exclaimed. (Phoebe is one of the only people I know who can actually *exclaim.*) "Are you going to write to him?"

I said I didn't know.

"You have to write to him," she said. "That letter is very nice."

After she left I looked at the envelope again and examined his address. I noticed that he lived on No. Catherine Street. I couldn't decide if that was a plaintive cry, as in: *There's no Catherine on this street!* Or an assertion: *No Catherine allowed!* I had too much time on my hands; I could see that.

But working with the materials at hand—and he was all I had—I wrote back. And he wrote back. He was lonely. He wanted me to visit him in the hills of Vermont. He would put me up in a hotel and would pay for it. He would introduce me to his son, who was the same age as my daughter. He was dear, he really was. And he was sorry, and he had changed. I remembered certain things. He was a very good kisser. He had a bright blue speck in his pale green eyes. I said I forgave him, and I thought I really did. I also thought I would be crazy to lay my heart on the line for him one more time, even if twenty-five years *had* passed and even if he *was* apologetic. I was discouraged. I wanted an Italian boyfriend and a good future. Instead, I had good mail and a forlorn guy who said *I'm sorry, I'm sorry, I'm sorry.*

A Lofty Experiment

$\mathcal{M}$eanwhile, Harper's not-returning-to-school declaration reverberated through our lives. Thomas, her father and my ex-husband and good friend, was as confounded as I was. Several of her friends from the Montessori school she'd attended through eighth grade went to an affluent and sophisticated private high school in Boston. Rose lived and went to school in Rhode Island, almost two hours from our house. No one we knew went to school in Six Mile Beach. As much as I loved Six Mile Beach, and I loved it deeply, the high school was widely—but falsely, it would turn out—believed to be substandard. School-related incidents appeared regularly in the town paper's police log. Someone slapped someone, someone shot someone with a paintball gun, stole a bike, made threatening calls, requested a restraining order. The drug-sniffing dogs were called in on a regular basis. We had never even considered sending her to school there. So when she'd graduated from middle school we'd gone to great lengths to send her to the cleaner, brighter public school in

the town I called Richer-than-Me, where Thomas lived. The
school she now wished not to attend.

I wasn't surprised. It didn't come out of the blue, and it
didn't shock me. The school in Richer-than-Me was full of
four hundred versions of the same kid, most of whom
wore polo shirts and excelled at sports. Harper wouldn't
be caught dead in a polo shirt, and her experience with
team sports was limited to a week-long, mornings-only
soccer camp when she was five. When I went to pick her
up on the first day, I looked for her in the swarm of little
kids running down the field. She wasn't there. She was
standing at the other end of the field using her red soccer
vest as a lens through which to see the world. Suffice it to
say that Harper was not a Richer-than-Me kind of girl. So
when she said, "I can't go back there," what I said was:
"You don't have to." I said it to the consternation of many,
including Thomas, my mother, most of my friends, some
of her friends, her guidance counselor, the superintendent
of schools, my therapist, and my ex-mother-in-law, who
said, "Can't she just go to school like a regular person?"

Well, she could, and she had, and now she wouldn't.
This decision didn't come as a surprise either. When I was
in high school my friend Bruce and I planned to buy a
farm and turn it into a school with no rules, kind of a
Summerhill with cows. Bruce drowned off Hawk's Nest
in the Long Island Sound on Christmas Day when we

were thirty years old, and we never did have that farm, but I never got over my rebel ideas about schooling. Thomas, on the other hand, was the product of as blue chip an education as was possible to come by, and was infinitely more conservative than I. But he came around because he joined me in one thing. He wanted the best for her, and sometimes that meant things he wasn't comfortable with.

Our children inform us. They teach us what they need. But independence is a complex matter. We had always encouraged hers, sometimes to a fault, but no one argued with the results. As one friend put it when Harper was eight, "My kids are kids. Your kid is a person." I had always listened to what she wanted and it had turned out well. When you decide to follow your child's instincts, you sometimes do things in ways other people think are mad.

Adding fuel to this fire, I am a fool for her need to learn. I am wildly idiotic with the desire that she have everything she wants and needs in the realm of knowledge. When she asks me if I will buy her a car when she turns sixteen, I say no. When she asks me if she can have a tattoo on the sole of her foot, I say, "Over my dead body." When she asks me for *knowledge*, I stand on my head to get it for her.

Which left us to figure out what she would do instead of returning to school in Richer-than-Me. We had two weeks until school started. She was over the suffering stage with the Italian boy, but still grieving for the summer college, for her fellow students, and for her teachers, particularly "Mr. Dave," her English teacher. All of the girls were in love with Mr. Dave. I had met him the day I came to pick her up. He was a normal-looking guy, portly, with receding hair.

"He must be thirty-five," I said.

"He's twenty-seven," she told me. "That's nothing."

It started out simply enough. When school started, she just didn't go. Instead, with the permission of the superintendent of schools, she cobbled together a complex plan of evening college courses, art classes, Latin, writing and literature, philosophy and art. She was peaceful and seemed happy enough about this plan, but I was worried. In theory we were embarking on a lofty experiment. In practice, I secretly thought we might founder. Then the art class was canceled, the evening college was tedious and far away, and although she never said so, I knew that our literary conversations couldn't hold a candle to those led by Mr. Ruggles, her tenth grade English teacher, who, apropos of an early-American story they were reading, once taught an entire class with a black veil over his head, and one day every year came to school in a long white dress. He got away with these eccentricities because he was a brilliant and gifted teacher, and once you have one of those, everyone else is pretty much toast in comparison.

So when Rose invited my daughter to visit her conservative Catholic school—I will call it A Deus—it seemed like a good way to spend one of our increasingly formless days, and to relieve my self-esteem from the battering it took every time I thought of Mr. Ruggles and his white dress.

For two years Rose had complained about the small (student body, one hundred and fifty) school housed in a mansion on some impressive acreage in a seaside town in Rhode Island. But after the summer college, which followed the same classical curriculum as A Deus, everything changed. Now the ethics and the philosophy and logic and Euclidian geometry all pointed in the direction of the best experience she had ever had, and at last, she was happy. But even she had some worries about Harper's arrival at the campus.

"What will you say if they ask you about gay marriage?" she asked.

"Let's hope that they don't," said my daughter.

The trip to A Deus was long, and Harper and I talked about all of our many and varied expectations of the school. Neither of us felt up to snuff. I'm not sure that we were exactly heathens or pagans, but both of us were all for gay marriage and neither of us fit the A Deus mold. Harper had scraped up an outfit that satisfied the draconian dress code, and I am embarrassed to say that I, who never wear skirts, had unearthed a serviceable one from my closet and put it on.

In spite of our preparations, I didn't feel Catholic enough, which, since I wasn't Catholic at all, was sign enough to me that I was on the wrong team. I was a pastiche of religious beliefs, I was pro-choice, and I swore, sometimes excessively. My daughter, however, seemed oddly comfortable in the headmaster's waiting room. She is far more open-minded than I, and has an inner poise that both of us suspect came from the Montessori school she attended for five years, because we know that it did not come from me. Within me lurked—in spite of my mild-mannered appearance and Volvo station wagon—the wild and dark-eyed shadows of my younger years, and I suspected that the headmaster would see them in my eyes.

He turned out to be a soft-spoken man in a crisp white shirt, sharply creased khakis, and red bow tie. Although he was slightly stilted in his mannerisms and speech, and referred to a pregnant colleague as being "with child," he was oddly personable and talked with a fond perceptiveness about even the most irascible of his students. I sat uncomfortably with my skirt and shadows, but I was impressed by that.

"Who are your favorite writers?" he asked Harper.

"F. Scott Fitzgerald and Dr. Seuss," she answered, and he laughed happily. Later I would find out that one student was an avid fisherman who ate raw clams or sea urchin roe for lunch. The school, it seemed, had its own share of eccentricity, which endeared it firmly to my heart.

After our brief interview he walked us downstairs to where the students were lined up neatly for lunch. Rose walked out to the car with us to get Harper's bag.

"Are my clothes okay?"

"The shirt collar is more than two inches below the collarbone, but you'll be fine." Rose's voice lowered to a whisper. "Did he ask you about gay marriage?"

I drove off in the Volvo, unaware that I had just entered a logistical nightmare that would reduce my estimated life span of ninety-three years to, let's say, a more manageable eighty-four.

Whatever Mr. Dave and the Catholic college had given Harper, she wanted more of it. She wanted Latin, the poetry of the ages, the great philosophical treatises, and, to both of our surprise and my dismay, she loved A Deus.

She loved the logic, the calm interweaving of philosophy and ethics into every aspect of the day. She knew the commute was too long, but she suggested on the phone from Rose's house, where she was spending the night, that if she were to go to A Deus, she could live with Rose's family during the week.

"The school year is only a hundred days," she said, anticipating my response.

"It's not going to happen," I said, and the conversation descended into an emotional roller coaster from which we didn't emerge for four weeks.

My first reaction was panic. *I'm going out there and I'm getting her back.* I actually had to restrain myself from driving the two hours, storming Rose's house, and seizing Harper as from the headquarters of a missionary. What drove my fear, it was obvious even to me, was the prospect of losing her.

My friend Sage talked me down. Sage was, as her name suggests, one of the wisest of my friends. She was a member of a group called the Moon Women—four of us who, for years, had met at the beach every full moon. Our moon days had passed, but I still relied on them, Sage and Scarlet and Martha, for wisdom on the frequent occasions when I had none.

"Give it a day," Sage said. But I didn't.

I was still agitated and angry, at Harper, at A Deus, at

the confusion and complication that had just entered my life. I was sure it was not a good idea, but I didn't want to end the night on a bad note, so I called Harper again. She picked up the phone.

"Hi," she said in a quietly pissed-off voice.

"I just called to say hello," I said.

"Oh," she said, tersely.

"That went well," I said bitterly. And then I hung up on her. I'm not proud of it.

I was raised under the religious auspices of a beautiful red stone Episcopal church in a small town in Connecticut. On Sundays my mother, with me and my brothers, Jack and Andrew, in tow, traipsed to town, went into the church, and sat in a pew. Girls wore hats. Boys wore ties. Upon sitting down, my mother would place her folded hands on the back of the pew in front of us, bow forward, and place her forehead against her hands. Her lips would move. She wore red lipstick and had black hair and was beautiful. Sometimes I would copy her. The folding of hands, the forehead against them. I had no idea what she was doing, but it was decidedly mysterious. Otherwise, I hated church. I sat still with great difficulty, as I still do. The minister was a priest and we called him Father, and we had Sunday school in the basement with a pinched-looking woman who once yelled at me for losing Jack, the younger of my brothers, at a school play. The high point of my Sundays was searching for the tiny old woman who wore a fox stole around her bony shoulders. If I sought her out after the service, she would let me pet it and touch its fake black eyes. This drove my mother crazy. After church people streamed up the small-town sidewalks, and in my memories of those days, it is always summer.

From that church I grew into what I thought might be a pantheist, or a Shinto, for whom even rocks have souls. But once I went to a special Catholic prayer service held for the dying mother of one of Harper's classmates, and we said the rosary over and over and over for hours, and I would have left except that it would have been awkward, so I stayed. Afterward, when I drove home and got out of my car and stood looking across the wet grass to the pond and the lights of the houses on the other shore, I felt expanded. I felt like a *lantern*. So I understood the attraction of A Deus and Harper's desire for the life of the mind combined with the life of the spirit because I shared it. Even Thomas, already torn by the shared custody arrangements necessitated by our divorce, understood. I admired him for that.

Still, A Deus took us by surprise. Faced suddenly with the prospect of either sending our daughter off to the imaginary clutches of what now seemed like a convent, or saying no to something we knew she wanted for all the right reasons, we felt propelled toward an impossible decision. We talked it through, working as well together as we had in a long time. We understood. We were willing to stretch. We were willing to let go. We were seized by a combined desire to accede to her wish to go back to school, and a strange, almost incomprehensible approval of the place she wanted to attend.

Even in the middle of this time of chaos and fear, I knew that there was a subtext to this situation in which we found ourselves. Our child was striving to leave, and we were striving to let her. The pulling and letting go had begun. I could see that. I wasn't ready.

When Harper came back from Rose's house, I took her to dinner at our favorite Indian restaurant and over the Peshawari nan and vegetable samosas I felt a distance already developing between us. She was polite and slightly proper. When I took one of the Lord's many names in vain during a routine traffic curse, I winced. I looked into the future and saw many weekend dinners ahead of us in which, returned from her school and Rose's family for the weekend, she would be polite and increasingly remote and I would, out of nervousness, swear more and more. I felt

awkward. We were never awkward. I felt nervous. That
had never happened before. The only thing that broke the
tension was the young Indian man named Omar and his
Caucasian friend, sitting behind us, who talked at length
about an acid trip they had taken in which the friend was
mesmerized by a ladybug dancing, he thought, on his be-
half. He also thought that his girlfriend had turned into a
salamander.

On the way home we drove down Six Mile Beach, to the
end of the peninsula. I stopped at the beach and stood on
the seawall watching the long white rows of waves coming in, one after another. She was, in the peculiar way
that our children are, the light of my life. But, I told myself, *I can do this*. Then I got back in the car just in time to
hear Al Green sing *Let's stay together*, the Zombies sing *Tell
her no*, and the Talking Heads sing *Love me till my heart
stops*. And I told her she could go.

And so, without giving it enough thought at all, I had
just told my irreverent daughter, to whom style meant so
many different things that there should have been as many
words for it as there are Inuit words for snow, that she
could live with our deeply conservative Catholic friends
for most of the week, nine months a year, and go to a rig-
idly Christian school, where *dress-code* was a verb, where

one student ate meals of small marine life out of Tupperware containers, and where, out of the thirty-student junior class there were five girls—three Marys, a Maria, and a Mariah—named after the mother of Christ.

The next day, my eyes opened to the fact that, although it was a wonderful and almost otherworldly school at which I knew she would be happy, the logistics were impossible, and that I wasn't—after all—ready to let her go. I knew that when she went off to wherever she would go after high school, it would be hard, but it would be possible. I would be sad, but I wouldn't feel like throwing up. It would be the right order of things. She wouldn't be fifteen.

I told her at the kitchen table among the remnants of our supper. I was peaceful and calm.

"It's too complicated," I said. And it was. I didn't go into the complex tangle of emotions that comprised the threads that held us together. I didn't go into the fact that I was not prepared for this.

"So," she said, sarcastically, "am I going to be able to go to *college?*"

The Difference Between
My Mother and Me

The A Deus fiasco shook my confidence. I was a good mother, but clearly I hadn't been firing on all cylinders in that decision-making process. My friends were either appalled that I had even considered letting her go or appalled that I had not, finally, done it. I was overprotective, was the message, and it was not a *new* message, and I knew that it was partly true. As a parent I seesawed between what I suspected was mostly unnecessary protection and allowing her to take risks. When I pondered my protective aspect, I thought of my mother, who had not been plagued by such worries, perhaps because she had three children. Someone once told me that when your first child drops her pacifier on the floor, you throw the pacifier away. When your second child drops the pacifier on the floor, you stick it in your mouth to clean the dirt off before returning to her. When your third child drops the pacifier you don't even notice. I was still throwing the pacifier away.

There were other differences between my mother and

me. The mysterious dark-haired woman I steadfastly re-member wearing a long white dress and carrying a wand was also the mother who chased my younger brother, the irascible Jack, around the garden with a broom when he failed to do his paper route and went off to play baseball instead. In spite of the white dress and wand, she was a worker, as was my older brother, the quiet and noble An-drew. I was cerebral. A thinker. A reflector. In fact, though I am embarrassed to say it, the quote under my high school yearbook picture was, "Reflection is the path of immortal-ity. Thoughtlessness is the path of death." When I told Harper that, she laughed for about ten minutes.

My mother was now eighty-two years old, and she ac-complished more in a day than I did in a year. She got up at dawn, drank two cups of strong black coffee, pointed her-self at some work, and went until it was done. We're not talking little old lady work. We're talking labor. On a 90-degree day the previous summer, she power-washed her house, her fences, her patio, all of her brick sidewalks, and the cement around her pool. And she was *gleeful* when she told me about it. Another day that week she dug up all of the plants and shrubs in a three-by-twelve-foot garden bed and trans-planted them to the other side of the house. Then she pur-chased several barrels of river rocks and wheelbarrowed them into the backyard, where she spread them around a shade garden that measured maybe twenty-five by fifteen feet. Then she left for vacation: a weeklong kayaking trip in Arizona and a drive to New Mexico, where she built book-cases and tackled her sister's unkempt yard before flying home to prepare the fall arrangements for her window boxes. A typical visit to *my* house involved an early morning arrival, coffee, and the purchase of tools. By midmorning she would be in the backyard with a pickax, hacking a gar-den out of my inhospitable, rocky soil.

She usually stopped at about five o'clock, had two stiff scotches, and went to bed early. And did some version of the whole thing all over again the next day.

Andrew was cut from the same cloth. In his spare time, he might figure out how to attach a plow to his tractor or draw up plans for a barn. If he built a box—not unusual—he would build a box so beautiful, seventeen people would want to buy it. Jack compared himself to Andrew, and I compared myself to my mother. We commiserated about it, but really, there was little comfort. The power-washing and kayaking and plow attaching and box making stood as if monuments of hard labor in comparison to Jack's and my intellectualism and more cerebral work ethic.

My friends found my mother amazing and wonderful. "Good for her!" they said. "What a great role model!" And don't get me wrong: I was grateful to have a mother who was independent and hardy and adventurous. But I was not like her. I didn't drink coffee, or scotch for that matter, but if I did, maybe I would have her energy. I would forge ahead. I would have a clean basement, the right kind of rake, and two hose caddies. I would have fixed that outdoor spigot months ago. I would plant my tomato plants on sunny windowsills in *February*. I would own a skill saw. If I were my mother I would not be sitting, in the middle of the day, in a leather recliner, reading.

I learned to smile when she drove by her friend's house and said, "I don't know what she does all day. Look at that house. It needs to be power-washed." I schooled myself not to wonder what she thought about my house and about me, whose work habits I suspected she understood as little as I did hers.

As the only girl, I felt I had carried a special mantle of expectation. I was not a girly girl, but I knew what they were. My friend Judy was a girly girl and so was her mother. Their house was painted pink. My mother was not a girly girl either, and I'm not sure she wanted one, but she might have wanted a girl whose heels did not rip out her hem stitches from kneeling down to look at the grass, and she might have wanted someone who could sit still, liked school and teachers, and worked up to her potential.

Mostly I read voraciously and taught myself. This went well enough, I suppose, though I now wish, too late, that I'd been more amenable to training.

In fact, my first literary life consisted of hiding from almost everyone the fact that I wrote *anything*. I showed my poems once to my friend Sue, who read the poems and showed them to her mother. They both loved them. They told me I was good. I never showed them to my own mother, whose job it was to do things like make me scrub from my face the lipstick I sometimes used as blush. I know in hindsight that she was doing me a favor, but I didn't see it that way then. I wanted a mother who would love my poems and let me smudge my cheekbones with lip gloss.

My mother reached out to me in the ways she could. She bought me a briefcase and a desk, and every Christmas my stocking brimmed with office supplies and notebooks. I know now what I did not know then: that she knew how my mind worked, and was feeding it. But by high school our relationship was tumultuous and adversarial, and we had no foundation to carry us through. I didn't *know* her. She didn't know me. I suspected we didn't like each other much, and we had no fun together. I still feel regretful about those years and the many years to follow when we couldn't traverse the chasm between us. The main difference between my mother and me was that she had a daughter who was as different from her as it was possible to be, and I had a daughter as familiar to me as daylight.

That is, of course, a double-edged sword. When your child is someone with whom your dinner conversation can range—one subject leading to the next in an uninterrupted free flow—from extraterrestrials to primordial ooze to quantum physics, to whether perception is necessary for reality, to Schrödinger's cat, to the Zen koan in which the disciple answers *mu* to the question of whether a dog has Buddha nature, to the nature of umami and the question of whether, before you knew that it existed, it was philosophically possible to taste it when you ate mushrooms—then it is hard to comprehend eating your homely dinner of a grilled cheese sandwich and tomato soup without her.

The Straw

By October, though matters of schooling took up quite a bit of my mental energy, so did Hunter. We had begun e-mailing regularly, and, while I felt wary of his neediness, I was compelled by my memories of him, the mingled remembrances of friendship and lust. I still felt caught between them even in my fantasies about him. Would we be able to resume as friends? I didn't think so. Would we be able to resume as lovers? More likely, but did I really want to? Our correspondence, from the beginning, lived right on that edge.

When I'd first known him, in graduate school, I lived in a tiny three-room attic apartment near Emily Dickinson's house, with a row of windows that looked over her church. He threw pebbles at my windows and drove me everywhere in his battered blue truck. Hunter had grown up there, in that sleepy farm town—and was as rooted as the trees along the wide river, and as beautiful. He showed me the trout farm where great blue herons patrolled the pools of fingerlings. He showed me the Polish farms owned by the parents of his childhood friends, where he could stop to say hello and come away with bags of green beans and tomatoes.

Hunter was wiry and strong and handsome: dark hair and those pale green eyes. As a friend he was stellar. He was attentive and funny. He told me he loved me because of the battered but tidy boots I'd bought for eight dollars a decade before, in New York City. He half lived in the woods. He'd once slept outside under a pile of dried leaves only to be woken in the night by a stag pawing at the ground around him. He took me fishing at the reservoir and we sat in our little aluminum rowboat and talked for hours, our lines dropped unattended into the water. Then there was a hatching, and tiny baby spiders, hundreds, maybe thousands, of them, floated out of the sky on little threads and dropped onto the water like snow. When we organized ourselves to leave, two eighteen-inch lake trout swam in lazy circles from our lines. Once I bought a goose at a farm auction and it lived at his house and swam in a little metal tub until it got too big. These were the kinds of things that happened when I was with Hunter. We walked for miles in the woods. We found arrowheads. We were attacked by a goshawk, and escaped, and were attacked again.

Now, twenty-five years later, he quickly became more and more interested. He would like it if I called him. He would like it if I came to visit him in the far city in which he now lived. He forgave me for not e-mailing him right away. I should do what I wanted. I should not apologize. He called me Buster. He called me his queen and hero. He said that the thing about fires was that you could start them again.

I was tempted. I harkened back to a time when I had been woken in the middle of the night by the phone and his reedy voice whispering "Marry me." So much time had passed. It seemed both crazy and perfectly reasonable that here he was again, saying *Buster*, saying *my queen and hero*.

I had loved that boy. I had worshipped him. Even if I *was* fifty-five, I wanted that happy-ever-after story, and it seemed like a good idea to have it with someone I'd already loved, someone whose big bed in a tiny room in a small house in the woods I'd already shared. It seemed simpler than starting fresh with someone new. And yet, I thought that if I told him we could start that fire again, it would only be a short matter of time before it went out. That was our pattern, and I, gun-shy, didn't see why it would have changed.

So I was not a good friend. I didn't answer his latest e-mail, the one in which he told me that a renewed relationship could work out. "You don't know that it won't," he said. "And I don't know that it will. But life is grasping at straws and maybe I want to grasp at this one." He was right. Neither of us knew. But I didn't want to be a straw to grasp at. As I recalled, both of our previous relationships with each other had begun when he was grasping at straws, and had ended when a better straw came along, a prettier straw, one who lived closer by, one who rode horses like a broncobuster or once beat Andre Agassi at Ping-Pong. So what if Andre hadn't been at the top of his Ping-Pong game. Still: a better straw. It usually didn't take long for the new straw to come along. Once he'd found the good straw, the exceptional straw, he would stay with her for quite a while. I was the temporary straw, the in-between straw, the transitional straw. I just hated that.

The prospect of being the lesser straw seemed, at my age, a painful thing to even contemplate. I was, postmarriage, leery enough to think that relationships would all end in failure. When I was younger, in the Hunter days and before, I was both blinder and braver. I was willing to dive, willy-nilly, into love. Marriage had left me wary. The fact that Thomas and I were pretty much best friends was wonderful, both for us and for Harper, but it did not inspire confidence in me. I wasn't sure what it said about my ability to make good relationship choices that a man whom I was absolutely incapable of living with was also someone I could not live without and didn't want to.

And so I didn't answer Hunter's e-mails. Or, in fact, I did answer him—letters long and short, e-mails contemplative or chipper—I just didn't *send* them. Sometimes I wondered if I would have felt differently if I was in better shape—buff, even—or had taken up horseback riding or competitive pool. Maybe. But maybe if those things had been true about me, I would have been the better straw to begin with. At any rate I wasn't, and really wasn't *going* to be. Ever.

Then he sent me a package. "Shit," I said, and pulled out two large and beautiful feathers.

"Tell me those are not from him," Harper said. I nodded. She grinned wolfishly and pointed her thumb at me.

"You still *got* it!" she said.

But I didn't. I didn't have it. My interest in men was rusty and disused. Maybe pheromone deficit had set in. Maybe it was that men, like women, lost something in the process of settling down. I didn't want to hear their stories of disappointment and I didn't want to tell mine. But I was not ready to let go of Hunter, either. If he thought of me as a straw to grasp at, I thought of him as the ace up my sleeve, some kind of secret or booby prize.

The wild girl I once had been, she ran with boys. I wanted her carelessness and courage. I wanted her back, and part of me wanted a love affair for her, a big, messy, something-to-live-and-die-for, smash-that-sucker-flat love affair. I thought of Picasso standing at the window waiting for Françoise, waiting with a kind of insistence, as if he could will her arrival. I thought of Françoise sweeping along the beach, Picasso following her, holding the umbrella. And I wanted that. I wanted the sweeping along the beach, someone willing my arrival, holding the umbrella.

Because I married late and had Harper late, I had, in her eyes, a vast previous life. Even as my present life had become over time less interesting to me, my past life took on a new importance to *her*. She was interested in the boyfriends I'd had in what I thought of as my misspent youth. To her, it seemed a wild and poetic youth, and really it might have looked that way, since I didn't tell her the half of it. To her I had been a great adventurer, a warrior in the realm of love.

The e-mails I finally resumed with Hunter were fun and exciting, if also confusing, to me, but not as fun and exciting as they were to her. And when I also began to correspond with Harold, another old boyfriend who once ran ten miles in a blizzard to see me, who had once invited me to Africa and who had wanted to marry me, the excitement increased exponentially. Harold even sent her a package. He told me it was coming but not what was in it, and when it arrived she ripped it open excitedly and extracted a battered orange T-shirt that had a large bleach mark on the back and an old poem of mine printed on the front. The poem was memorable for its mediocrity and for the brevity which had allowed it to be printed on a T-shirt by a business that was now, I was sure, defunct. She held it up and read the poem, then quickly took it up to the lair of her attic bedroom. As if it were a pearl of great price that I, given half a chance, would snatch away and keep for myself, even though Harold was long in my past and had been married for twenty years since I last saw him.

She wanted stories, about my days in Cambridge, my poet days, my second literary life, the days "in which such music could be written," in which I smoked cigarettes and drank wine, published in small esoteric journals, lived in a series of attic studios, and made very little money. I was in a few different writing groups, in the best of which two dark-skinned men and I smoked, praised each other's poems, and laughed. I told her about my friend Shep who lived in an abandoned warehouse with three ancient letter presses. I told her about the Velvet Underground, the Talking Heads, Brian Eno, and Kurt Schwitters. And later, when she followed her own path from Byrne to Eno to Schwitters, she cornered me in the kitchen.

"Dude," she said, joking, "you were a part of the underground."

I wasn't. She knew it and I certainly did, but it was her

way of letting me know that she was bowing to me, and to the myth of my glorious past.

Back in the days when I first knew Hunter and the boy with the coffee-colored skin, I'd had a teacher who'd been a nun for twenty years before leaving the convent to become a poet. She wrote things like: *The bells of the Angelus pour down the valley: Angelus Domini nuntiavit Mariæ*, and told me once, in her book-filled office in the trees, that she had a fantasy of my life as being like that of Amandine-Aurore-Lucie Dupin, also known as the writer George Sand, who'd had many lovers among painters and writers and was the mistress of Chopin. I sat with my teacher in the dappled sunlight, not knowing what to say. I couldn't say it wasn't true, because it wasn't so far from it, and I couldn't say it *was* true because it was so outlandish. So for a while I didn't say anything, and neither did she.

Hipper-than-Me

In early October, here's where we stood in matters of schooling. A Deus was not an option, and Six Mile High School was out of the question. There were some good kids there, I knew that. There were kids who went to Harvard and Yale and MIT, but we had, after all, started out with something lofty in mind, and a rough school surrounded by lobster boats did not seem to be it. Thus was born our next brilliant idea.

For years, Thomas had wanted to move to the town in which he worked, an hour away in good traffic, a town with one of the best school systems in Massachusetts, one town away from Cambridge, where he and I had lived for much of our adult lives. And it seemed serendipitous, actually, these two things converging, his desire to move and our need for a good school. So he decided that he *would* move, the plan being that Harper would commute from Six Mile Beach to school in Hipper-than-Me, where the children of MIT professors took immersion Spanish and advanced choral technique and there were seventeen art class offerings and eight separate sections of *badminton*.

Hipper-than-Me was a small, bucolic, yet curiously urbane town where grown men in baggy shorts sat at café tables in midday typing away at their laptops, and interesting-looking teenagers slouched along the streets: a boy with heavy metal blaring from his earphones; a girl with dreadlocks; a boy with braids. The school was huge, with a student body of four thousand and a campus the size of a college. In contrast, I lived in a town in which there *were* no urbane men with hairy legs and laptops, and no café tables for them to sit at—no cafés at all, for that matter—and Harper's middle school graduating class had consisted of fourteen students.

Then things happened with alarming speed. One week after we settled on this plan, Thomas had rented a house in Hipper-than-Me, packed up his house in Richer-than-Me and moved. I enrolled Harper in the public high school, where we were shown around the vast campus by an unsmiling woman named Mrs. Hatchet.

Afterward, we stopped at Thomas's office to pick up the key to his new house so that Harper could show me her rooms. His was a small house on a quiet road in a pleasant and modest part of town. It had a slightly neglected feel—in a good way—and reminded me of my grandparents' house in the middle of the woods, where pine needles fell on the path and chipmunks skittered along the stone walls. As if to cement this impression, the driveway was littered with pine needles and a chipmunk scampered quickly across them. Harper inserted the key into the lock.

"It doesn't work," she said.

We drove back to his office.

"I'm so sorry," he said. He handed over another key.

This one did not work either.

On the second time out of the driveway I backed my new car into the mailbox, incurring a deep scratch. I cried bitterly for just a moment.

"This is a bad sign," Harper said.

"No, it isn't," I said, but I was lying.

On the third try we made it inside and I discovered that Thomas had rented a perfect house. It had a loftlike upstairs landing and a boatlike bedroom, closets the size of Manhattan, and a bathroom the size of my bedroom. And all of this, the entire second floor, was Harper's. At the sight of this space, even I wanted to live there and I could see those rooms growing more and more appealing as Harper's life in Hipper-than-Me took hold.

We returned the third key to Thomas, and on the way out of his office building we followed an extremely old couple as they tottered down the hall. They were both tiny, about five feet tall. He preceded her, in a walker.

"Maybe I'll take these two home," he chortled as he shuffled past Harper and me.

"You can't have him," she said. "He's mine."

I held the door open for them.

"Take your time," I said.

"Come on, Chollie," she said. And then she said to us, "This is how I do it," and hit him in the butt with her pocketbook.

I was enchanted by "Chollie" and his ancient butt-whacking wife, but I also felt a sudden melancholy. Thomas and I were probably way too close for a divorced pair to be. We had decided when we separated that we would continue to be a family, and we had succeeded. We had kept our word and had not faltered. But we would never be this very old couple walking down the hall, and this would be the first time in twenty years that we would live more than five minutes apart.

The next day, although it made no sense, Harper packed every piece of clothing she owned. Every dress, every shirt, every pair of jeans, every sweater, shoe, and boot. Then she packed all of her jewelry. Not a necklace, ring, or bracelet remained. Every cosmetic, hair product, skin cream, nail polish, eyeliner, lipstick, hair clip, tie, and bobby pin. I was hurt. She could, I thought, have left a pair of jeans and a T-shirt, a few necklaces, a pair of earrings.

Then I took her out to lunch. And for some reason that

I do not understand, as we sat across from each other in the booth and ate our salads, I started to tell her about my great-grandfather, about his madness and his search for the place where he would strike it rich, and the many countries to which he took his wife and nine children. I told her how, on the boat to Argentina, a rich couple fell in love with one of his daughters, Rose, and wanted to buy her, but my great-grandmother wouldn't let him sell her. And how, when Rose suddenly fell mysteriously ill at the end of the voyage, he took her to the hospital, and they never saw her or the rich couple again. I told her about how he once became jealous of a distant farmer and set out to shoot him, and how my great-grandmother sent her daughter, my grandmother, Harper's namesake, ten miles across the backcountry of fields and hills, on horse-back, to warn him.

Our plan called for Harper to live only a few days a week with Thomas. But, shortly *after* Thomas packed up his life and moved, Mrs. Hatchet at the high school belatedly informed us that in order to go to school in Hipper-than-Me, Harper would have to live there full-time. And though we wanted her to go to a good school, and Thomas would have been delighted to have her with him, this option felt impossible to all of us. I would have to move, part- or full-time, to Hipper-than-Me. I would have to leave the cottage I had rebuilt two years earlier and in which I had started my new life. I would have to rent it out or sell it, or use my meager earnings as a writer and my savings to support a second home. Thomas and I concocted a Byzantine plan whereby this would be possible, a veritable black hole of here, there, rent, chicken-sitters, and roommates. I knew that none of this was a good idea. But I could not, day after day, say the magic words that would stop the runaway train in its tracks. I could not say, *There is a perfectly good school in Six Mile Beach.* I couldn't say it because I didn't believe it was true. I would turn out to be both right and wrong about that.

My inability to say these words went beyond my desire for her to take advanced choral technique and immersion Spanish. I didn't especially love Hipper-than-Me, but part of me wanted to pack up my life and work and move. I would get a little pied-à-terre. I would have the best of both worlds: the comfort and beauty of Six Mile Beach and the *hip* of Hipper-than-Me. I would get proximity to poetry readings, galleries, the repertory theater, lectures by esoteric philosophers, and the exhibition of artists' sketchbooks now showing at the Fogg. Plus, I wanted to decorate the pied-à-terre.

Wikipedia says that a pied-à-terre is a "small second home with connotations of a jet-set lifestyle," and that they "are usually decorated very well." I would live up to that. I would buy a piece of art I had seen in the exhibition room at my daughter's new school, and a standing wooden Buddha I had seen in a discount shop that carried a surprising number of weird hokey chicken items and an equally surprising number of lovely Buddhas. I would decorate in a lighter, freer way, and the space would be quirky but airy, with vaulted ceilings and skylights and a large scrubbed pine table situated at one end of the huge living room, covered with neat stacks of books and a tiny basket for keys. I began to long for this space and its dinner parties and poets. I felt myself shedding some kind of skin. The skin of the homemaker and false suburban housewife was sloughing off, and I felt energized by the new skin under the old one and the scales that began to drop from my eyes.

And yet, as I drove down Six Mile Beach to the very end of the peninsula, I looked at the water—everywhere you go in Six Mile Beach there is water—and I felt my heart expand. I didn't know what my new life in the pied-à-terre in Hipper-than-Me would be like, but I knew it wouldn't be like this. It wouldn't be blue and windblown. It wouldn't taste like salt.

On a Monday in mid-October, I started looking for the loftlike space and my daughter started school in Hipper-than-Me. On Tuesday we discovered the savings intended to support the pied-à-terre were insufficient. And without that money, the plan would not work. The remaining option was one that none of us had ever envisioned taking. There was only one choice left: the public high school in Six Mile Beach, a brick building at the end of the peninsula, right next to the windmill, bordered on three sides by water and around which three-hundred-foot tankers routinely passed on their way to the ocean. On Tuesday, we left Hipper-than-Me and went home.

Our house in Six Mile Beach was cold and the furnace was broken. I started a fire in the woodstove and made pasta with olive oil and salt for dinner. On Thursday I drove Harper to Six Mile High School. There, she started a new school for the second time in a week, and I watched her walk in. She did not complain. True to form, she walked into the school with her head up. I had never thought much about courage or realized how much of it she had.

Then I drove back down the long road that ran through Six Mile Beach like a vein, from the narrow and treacherous strait called the Gut, through the point of the peninsula, past the Coast Guard station, through the village, over the land spit, through the alphabet streets arranged backward, past the tiny commercial center with its green-painted storefronts, across the length of Six Mile Beach, and home to the little house by the salt pond, nine hundred feet from the ocean, from the black rocks of Black Rock Beach, from the place where water poured over the seawall and waves broke over the cottages in winter storms. We were home again, in the place of mist. In the place where the sun rose over France and moved across an entire ocean to light up the white houses on all the hills of this town. The journey we set out on, the one that was meant to take us to a rarefied place where poets and philosophers dwelled, had spun us out of control and spat us out again, stunned and disbelieving, on these windswept and rocky shores.

Part Two

Other Forms of Leaving

Beached

Every morning I drove Harper down Six Mile Beach to the high school, drawn like a thread on a needle. I let her off with her fellow students and then I commenced to fear. Every morning a gaggle of well-dressed teenagers stood at the dock across from the high school and waited for the ferry to take them into Boston to their private school on a good city street where they took classes in figure drawing and philosophy. I felt, I confess, shaken by the fact that Harper was not one of them. I discovered that I was an educational snob. I could do homeschooling. I could do esoteric. I could do upscale private. I could almost do conservative Catholic. I had a hard time, it appeared, doing Six Mile Beach.

I was in shock from the past month, I knew that. In four weeks Harper had landed in three schools in three towns, I had cried me a river, every door on earth had been slammed in my face by whatever the powers of the universe were, and now I was afraid of everything. I was afraid that she would hate it there, that she would find no like minds, that she would regret our decision. But we had no other choice. All of the brilliant ideas had been used up. This was as good as it was going to get. There was no Plan D. But every day, immediately after I dropped her off—and school started very early—I woke up Sage or my mother or Jack or Thomas and began my litany of things that could go wrong.

"I think this is going to be all right," said Sage.

"She's going to be fine," said Thomas.

"You need a job," said my mother.

The whole school experience had left me reeling with surprise and confusion. In my desire to do the best for her, I had, in my eyes, failed. In the months to come, as I came to understand the new nature of my motherhood and my evolving relationship with Harper and the different lives awaiting both of us, I would reflect often on the school decisions that had seemed, at the time, driven by education, but were also, I came to see, sifted through the coming separation that neither of us could, at the time, fathom.

Slowly, our lives stabilized. Six Mile High School was a dichotomy. There were ruffians, knuckleheads, fighters, theater geeks, jocks, and children of upscale bankers and physicians, with all of whom Harper found a slightly discomforting community. Six Mile High School was, I would come to learn, a good school trying valiantly, and mostly succeeding, to serve a varied community. In the beginning, though, because Harper started late, the classes available to her were too easy. She had virtually no homework. Instead she devoted herself at home to painting and astrophysics. She showed me photographs from the Hubble Space Telescope. They were terrifying in their mysterious beauty. They made me believe in God, Brahma, Krishna, Shiva, and every immortal inhabitant of Mount Olympus. I, in turn, told her about an astrophysicist named Dickie Plum, a childhood friend of mine who once turned the insides of an apple into juice without breaking its skin and then left it, all shiny and bright, on the desk of our earth science teacher.

As for me, I cleaned my house and ordered the winter's firewood. I watched the chickens putter about their yard. I pulled up the remains of my vegetable garden and mowed the lawn for what I hoped was the last time of the season. I tied a tarp over the lawn mower so that it wouldn't blow away during the fierce winter storms of Six Mile Beach. I finished moving the pile of mulch that had been sitting in my driveway since July. The pile of mulch was then replaced by a pile of wood that took me four days to stack. I was home.

For my soul resided in Six Mile Beach. The learning curve here had been steep for me. This was the first house I had owned by myself. It was the first house I had renovated. It was the first house whose expansive lawn I had sole responsibility for. And I was proud of those things, proud of the tool shed I'd finally bolted to the side of the house after it had blown down the outside basement stairs twice, proud of the raised beds, the vegetable garden, and the pretty white fence that masked the chain link of the chicken run. I was proud of the tools I had amassed: the tin snips, the palm sanders, the three different kinds of hammer, the complete set of wrenches, the vast array of drill bits, screwdrivers, work gloves, and garden tools. I was proud of the gas-powered Weedwacker and of the fact that I had never lost the key to my lawn mower.

I was proud of the town, too, of its beauty and its quirky citizens. Someone once described Six Mile Beach as "an interesting place, made up of townies, weird people who were left behind in the hippie revolution of the 70s, and more restraining orders than toilet paper." Once I stopped at a traffic light next to a hole-in-the-wall bar in front of which three weathered men, who had seen better and more sober days, sat drinking beer in battered wooden chairs in the early afternoon of what had been a sweltering day in a drought-ridden summer.

"I wish it would rain," said one.

"Jesus, I wish it would goddamn rain," said the second.

"I wish it would rain like a fucking bastard," said the third.

Six Mile Beach was in a class by itself.

But, though I was glad to be home, I grieved the loss of my imaginary urbanity: the pied-à-terre, the poetry readings, the intellectual discussions about art and literature, the company of other writers and like-minded souls. I had looked forward to that, though it would have been a consolation prize for doing something I hadn't really wanted to do. My friend Ed, dead these many years, once told me that when you give something up, you get something, and when you get something, you give something up. I had gotten my home back, my peace of mind, my daughter. I had given up Hipper-than-Me, the airy loftlike space, and the poets. You have to make choices in your life and, years before, I had chosen to leave Cambridge and its lofty environs and move here to this unassuming place surrounded by water. I had given up one thing and gotten another.

For a minute there, I had thought I could have both. The image of that life in Hipper-than-Me would stay with me in the months to come—the allure of the streets, the ability to walk to the market with a little string bag, to the library, to the small movie theater with its new independent movies, the town with cafés and hairy-legged men with laptops. I wondered what track our lives, Harper's and mine, would have taken if I had stayed in Cambridge those many years ago. I wondered if I would, someday, go back.

Philosopher Kings: Professor Lupin, the Werewolf, and I

I admit that not a small part of the appeal was the hairy-legged men. It was ironic that I lived in a town that probably had the highest percentage rate of single men in all of Massachusetts, but you might not want to date many of them. Not that it mattered much. Because none of us, in this house of females—two humans, a cat, a dog, and two chickens—was hormonally balanced: one in midlife, one a teenager, two spayed, and two terribly confused about whether or not I was actually a rooster. As for me, maybe the lust days were over. Maybe I had gone over that hill. Perhaps I *was* a Shinto priest, or should become one. I thought about whether I had any love drive left. I thought about whether I cared enough to try.

My distrust of Hunter had origins not only in our mutual past, but in my more recent history as well. I was convinced, postdivorce, that whoever I chose, however he seemed in the beginning, would turn out to be wrong.

Most of my friends were or had been divorced and, to my knowledge, none of them were dating. Women's magazines teemed with articles on finding new mates, but according to my limited surveys, the desire was wildly overestimated. My friend Christopher told me that after his first marriage, which began and ended when he was in college, he, too, found it impossible to imagine succeeding in love.

"I would see someone in the supermarket," he said. "She would be in front of me in the checkout line, and we would date, be married, and get divorced before my food even hit the counter."

He did date eventually, live with her, marry her, and have a baby. And although he once bought himself a table saw instead of a diamond ring for her, they seemed to be happy. They had been together a long time, but I had no idea how he made it past the checkout line.

I had married Thomas in my late thirties, after my free-wheeling youth. He was younger than I, terribly handsome, funny, irreverent, and responsible. We married after a two-year courtship, and I confess that I was more ready than he. I was sure I wanted children and he wasn't sure that he wanted them right away. But on the day I found out I was pregnant, before I even told him, he walked into the house and said, "I just saw this guy with two little kids, and I thought, you know, I want to do that."

Having Harper was everything either of us had hoped. Thomas whistled around the house—I had never heard him whistle before and have never heard him whistle since. He was a good father and a good husband, but as the years went by we did less well together, and then less well, and then even less, until, in spite of what was a deep regard for each other, we decided to go our separate ways.

I hadn't had (and hadn't wanted) any dates since my divorce, but I'd had one imaginary relationship with a zookeeper I'd had a crush on for a few months during my marriage, back when Harper was seven and he came to her school with an aardvark and two boa constrictors. He was short, somewhat heavy, and balding, I presumed, for I had never seen him without a baseball cap on. He had pockmarked skin and wore rumpled clothes that in a very generous stretch might be called shabby. He had pale blue eyes and a soft voice, and was one of those men who, in spite of the fact that they are not handsome, manage to be very attractive.

A couple of years after my divorce, I saw him at the

wildlife center where three days a week Harper fed baby birds—with their terrifyingly transparent bodies and giant heads—and I was pleased.

"How do you like living in Six Mile Beach?" he asked.

"I love it," I said.

"I live there now, too," he said.

The devious wheels spun in my head. He hadn't said "we."

"When did you move?" I asked.

"A few months ago," said he. "Where do you live?"

I told him, but I could see that he did not know the place I was referring to, because most people in Six Mile Beach don't know that where I live exists.

"How about you?" I asked.

"At the foot of Fort Hill," he said. Fort Hill was one of the two pricier parts of Six Mile Beach, and there were houses there that I coveted, but I didn't know about the foot of it. I could have asked, but I didn't. I had been thrown into panic by the thought that he might no longer be married.

Phoebe was my age, and single. Sitting at the edge of the huge ancient swimming pool in her backyard, between her house and the neighboring woods, I told her the story.

"Oh," she said in a fluttery sort of way, "you have to do it. You have to invite him over."

"Really?" I said. "Would you?"

"Oh, no," she said, horrified. "I wouldn't, but you should. Where does he live?"

"At the foot of Fort Hill."

"Ohhh," she said. "Very nice."

"Probably in one of those apartment buildings," I said.

"Those are kind of run-down," she said. "But ask him anyway."

I didn't get in touch with him, but we had a short imaginary relationship in which we began by having dinner at his apartment—one large room, like a loft, but less chic—in one of the dilapidated apartment buildings. I suggested a Zen-like be-in-the-moment relationship, a let-go-of-attachments kind of thing. Even in fantasy I was unable to commit. Why? Because he came with baggage.

Like I didn't? A woman of fifty-five with an ex-husband, a fifteen-year-old daughter, a dog, a cat, two chickens, and a tiny house with a flooding basement? A friend told me about a friend of hers, around my age, similar demographics, who was dating a man and really liked him. He drank too much, smoked cigarillos compulsively, and occasionally wore long cotton skirts, but only at home. But she *really liked him* and she was willing to live with all that. What could I live with? I wondered, since it appeared likely that, even in my imagination, I was going to have to live with something.

My imaginary relationship took somewhere between an hour and a day to play out in its entirety, and after it ended I sank into a mild gloom. When I told my friends about the imaginary breakup, they were comforting. They listed all the things about me that they cherished. They rolled their eyes at my response, which was, "But I'm out of shape, and I don't know how to dress."

"Look at him," they told me. "You've never even seen the top of his head."

After the imaginary date I fell in love with Remus Lupin, the new professor of Defense against the Dark Arts in the movie version of *Harry Potter and the Prisoner of Azkaban*. (When you have offspring who were seven when the first Harry Potter book came out, you tend to have read the whole series, and though Harper had read them all without my help, I was as big a fan as she.) I had liked Lupin well enough in the book, but on film he was *really* compelling. He was rumpled and weary, wore baggy, unfashionable clothes, and seemed unathletic. I could relate to that, being rumpled and weary and unfashionable myself. But Lupin was wise and kind and unafraid, a good balance, I thought, to my wisdom, anxiety, and fear. More important, he looked as if he might like to cook. He might like to muddle about my kitchen making soup, wearing his misshapen and colorless sweater. I did notice, however, that his pale, kind-looking face was marked with the thin lines of scars.

Unfortunately, I had forgotten that about two-thirds of the way through the book and movie, Lupin turned into a werewolf. And the movie made abundantly clear what the book had not: he was not your familiar werewolf, scary but predictable, hair breaking out on the arms, fangs, a crazed look taking over the pale gray eyes. No, Lupin was a really vile, hairless, ghoul-like werewolf, tall and attenuated, like a bad alien, something you've never seen before or imagined. Something really disgusting that you would find hard to forget in the morning.

Oh, I thought, *that's where the scars come from.*

If I had remembered his condition at the movie's outset, would it have changed what I felt? Would I have drawn back from the relationship before it even got off the ground? Would I have forgiven the werewolf to get the guy?

This is what I thought about when I thought about Hunter and other potential mates. I thought about the werewolf. Like my imaginary date, Hunter was now bald. Or balding. He told me he shaved his head and sent me a picture to prove it. I have to say that I liked him better with hair, but I couldn't really remember what that looked like because after our second breakup I had destroyed the only picture I'd had of him. I still had a picture of our goose.

Matronly, or, Washed Up, Part Deux

$\mathcal{W}$hen my first book was published, I imagined that a somewhat glamorous life would now be mine, possibly a Hipper-than-Me sort of life, one in which having the BlackBerry would be a necessity and trips to New York on the Acela would be commonplace. Instead, in the introduction to its excerpt of my book, *O, the Oprah Magazine* referred to me as a suburban matron. I must say that this rankled, and now, along with being washed up, the last straw, and sans pied-à-terre, I found that it rankled even more. I talked it over with a few people, including my agent, my publisher, my family, my neighbors, all my friends, and every patient audience I ever read to.

"Do I *look* like a suburban matron?" I'd ask.

"No," they would chorus, though I did tell them first that that was the correct answer. Yes, I wore linen shirts and owned some gold jewelry and drove a Volvo station wagon. The car in itself was an ominous sign, unless you had ever looked into it and seen the variety of dirt, farm implements, broken window screens, and old coats. (One of the mothers at my daughter's Montessori school once blurted out, "Could you *fit* anything else in there?" She was an interesting woman, a writer, and definitely more stately than I. I don't know what kind of car she drove, but I am relatively certain that the inside of it didn't look like a shopping cart.) I didn't think that anyone who once had to put a dollar in a jar for every time she swore in front of her toddler qualified for suburban matronhood, but in the face of my new and embarrassing jealousy of the as yet unwritten story of my daughter's future, I foundered in the vision of myself as a matron, a used-up matron at that, probably soon to be an old woman in a shiny-eyed fox stole.

In addition to the suburban matronhood, my new literary life, which had begun with the publication of my first book, also included a fair bit of worrying about what I looked like. Was I thin enough? Were my teeth white enough? And what about my clothes? When you have a beautiful daughter you become, as by an act of God, less pretty. And so, in addition to becoming less smart—as parents of teenagers do—your beauty days are essentially over. I was getting older, and so were all of my friends. The thinnest among us had widened ever so slightly, though Scarlet·

had recently lost quite a bit of weight. Even Andrew, who had so little body fat that even in salt water he sank like a stone, had given up desserts because he was getting a belly unseen by all but him. Personally, I love the Olympic swimmers with their seal-like layers of fat. But let's face it, for most of us, the Olympics are over.

The truth was, I was overweight, middle-aged, and my skin would never be the same. Now, I vowed, I would use moisturizer and I would stop eating poorly. Fortunately, I wasn't a complete disaster. I drank plenty of water, ate three meals a day, and my blood pressure was low. I was proud of that blood pressure. When I went for my physical, I shut my eyes while the nurse weighed me, and then vanity kicked in as soon as the blood pressure cuff came out. So the pressure was good, but everything else was going downhill.

"Starvation is the new diet," said Scarlet, and she wasn't kidding around. Like most American women I had always thought I had too many pounds, even when I didn't. I remembered a few times when I was unconcerned about weight, or concerned but not in a serious way, once because I was running eight miles a day and doing karate five times a week, and was *cut* for the first and only time in my life. Even so, I had worried a little, because I was badly addicted to Mystic Mints and slept with a box of them by my bed. The last time I had been at a reasonable weight, one I liked, was right after I took Harper to Disney World when she was seven and then I'd had the stomach flu for a week. Even then I hadn't been sure how I felt about bathing suits.

I had married someone who lived to exercise and enjoyed eating unadulterated tofu and kale. With him, I felt that I should have eaten only salad for the rest of my days, but instead I steadfastly gained weight for the entire time we were together. I thought of it now as unhappiness weight. The weight I gained *after* our separation, I thought of as freedom weight. Now I had finally reached the point where the weight was annoying me. I had finished my freedom gaining and arrived at "This has got to stop."

So I put the dog and the cat on a diet.

Let me explain the circuitous logic by which I arrived at this step. My dog, Sam, typically came out the back door at flying speed and leaped from the top of the deck stairs to the ground without touching any of the six actual stairs themselves. She landed running at breakneck speed for the nearest rabbit. But one time she hurt her knee upon landing and walked with a limp for a while. Following some bizarre reasoning, *she* was injured so *I* stopped exercising. At the time it didn't seem like an odd decision at all.

Now on their diets, Sam and Monkey lost weight. They really both needed to: Sam had been on prednisone for an allergy and had become crazed for food, a food maniac, and somewhere along the line Monkey had become a dumpling. A few days into the diet, Monkey was exhibiting signs of life. Sam was just herself, a hooligan, obsessed with small rodents. Rabbits, voles, moles, and mice: none were safe. I could tell she was not happy about the dog food limitations, but what with the rodents, she was definitely getting enough protein.

I, on the other hand, eyed the Weight Watchers manuals suspiciously and resented a dieting friend when she proudly told me that she had eaten seven almonds and an apple for lunch. I made resolutions, much like the ones I'd made when I'd tried to quit smoking eons ago and had written "death" on all my cigarettes every night before I went to bed, and then threw them away and bought new ones in the morning. I would start eating well tomorrow, I thought.

But the next day a package arrived in the mail. I thought it was a painting Hunter had said he would send to me, packed in an orchard box, or maybe even a box full of bear claws and hawk bones, such as he used to send me. It was from Hunter, all right, but it actually *was* an orchard box, from an actual orchard, and in it were two apples, a bottle of maple syrup, and a container of buttermilk pancake mix.

I was standing there, checking the abysmal calorie content of my maple syrup, when the phone rang and, as if to simultaneously offer me a consolation prize, break me out of my writer's solitude, and hand me my head on a platter, an old friend, Harper's godfather, a writer named Danny, called me up and invited me to New York to visit his writing group.

I had wished for urbanity and here it was. Be careful what you wish for.

New York, Real and Imagined

Although New York City is a place in which I have lived more than one imaginary life, in actuality I had been there only twice in the past twenty years. Even as I write that, I feel it must be a lie, so strong are the artificial memories of my halcyon days in lower Manhattan. If the life I did not have in Hipper-than-Me was urbane, you really cannot even imagine the abandon of some of those New York City lives.

Both of the *real* visits had been required of me by the publication of my book: one trip to meet my agent, the other to meet my publisher. When you are a middle-aged person who lives the sort of life that leads you to write a book with the word *chickens* in the title, the publishing world seems cloaked in mystery and sophistication. With no prior experience, I conjured up all kinds of strange, but compelling, possibilities.

My agent is a lovely and elegant woman with the mind of an editor and the literary eye of an eagle. She has a somewhat raspy, kind, but no-nonsense voice, which—based on our initial strictly telephone-based relationship—had led me to imagine her as an archetypal agent, a dark-haired, crepuscular person of small stature and large presence. When I first visited her I easily found her office building on Fifth Avenue and Thirty-fifth Street, but misread the floor number. Instead of ending up on the twentieth floor, I ended up on the second, a warren of janitorial rooms, dank hallways, and no windows. This worried me, though it confirmed, somewhat, my belief in the crepuscular agent. I finally figured out that I *was*, in fact, on the janitorial floor and ascended to the light-filled offices on the twentieth, with their huge high windows overlooking all of the rooftops in Manhattan. My agent turned out to be tall and charming and wore leopard-print glasses, which I coveted then and still covet. It took me several months to reconcile the actual agent with the imaginary one. For a while, I had both of them, one real, one imagined, until slowly the archetype faded away.

I didn't make the same mistake twice. Before I visited my publisher for the first time, I made her send me a photograph.

Because of those brief visits, both of which also fueled the BlackBerry craving, I could find my way around the city. I had an extremely cool pop-up map that I prized inordinately, so much that I actually hated to use it, and I *adored* the simple constancy of New York streets and avenues. Plus I was, after all, with Danny, who'd lived there for decades. I'd known him since childhood, so I was comfortable as skin with him, but I was not urbane and had no comfort level with five-star restaurants or with famous authors such as the ones in whose company I now found myself. I won't say who they were, but you would recognize their names.

In time there were seven or eight of us around a table laden with Middle Eastern finger food and several bottles of wine. There was a man as thin and ethereal as a ghost and a woman as dark and somber as a raven. Another man had heavily lidded eyes and a puffed up chest and looked the women up and down like a satyr. One woman had long thin fingers riddled with silver rings, and on that basis alone, I wanted to *be* her. A tall skinny man watched the whole thing as if from afar, his long legs stretched out, sockless ankles crossed casually.

Now, I am not exactly socially awkward, but in that crowd I was. I immediately felt that I did not qualify for the rarefied atmosphere. Danny was homey and voluble, as he is wont to be, a cheerful and enthusiastic conversationalist. But the rest of the conversation around the now-crowded table was conducted in the shorthand of people who have known each other well, for a long time, and have shared a common language, although they did not necessarily seem to like each other all that much. A waiter hovered. She knew who they were, too, and I could tell she had a manuscript somewhere that she was itching to give to one of them.

As if on cue, a man with a face like the business end of an ax, who had been dropping important literary names as if they were bread crumbs in the wilderness of lesser writers, *Mailer* this, and *Morrison* that, and *When I was on Oprah* lahdeedah, half-turned to the hovering young waiter. "I've had your manuscript for far too long," he said in a witheringly dismissive, patently fake tone, designed to let the waiter know, quite clearly, that he hadn't read it, was never *going* to read it, and knew *without* reading it that it was not worthy of his time.

I found myself wondering how Danny had gotten himself hooked up with these people.

I had brought a copy of my book for Danny, and it was passed hand to hand, the cover examined, the jacket copy read. The titular chickens may have been enough to discredit it from serious consideration, but it was also clear that the one thing that didn't happen at these meetings was anything resembling enthusiasm for one another's books. In fact, one's own book might not be as good if you said something good about someone else's. It was a parsimonious company in which I found myself, and I found that although I had looked forward to it with enthusiasm, this taste of urbane New York City literati made me long for Six Mile Beach, where my literary life consisted of being feted by the Garden Club and being the subject of an article in the local paper in which the accompanying photograph made me look like I had three chins.

On the way to Penn Station, Danny gave me the rundown on everyone.

"Who was that tall man with the white hair? The one who didn't speak?"

"Oh, that's X," he replied, giving the name of an author of three books I would have been proud to have written, a writer with a deep and lovely command of story and character and voice. My love for him was deepened by the fact that his books were set in the Paris of the Resistance. I couldn't believe I had missed the chance to tell him how much I admired him.

We passed a huge chain bookstore. "Look," Danny said, pointing to the front display window, where there was an eight-foot poster of the man with the elegant legs. He was beautiful, and I wanted him. We went inside and I bought three of his books and carried them home on the train as if they were treasures, which, in fact, they turned out to be.

The Parisian House Chicken

The day after I returned from New York, plunged from the literary world back into the world of Six Mile Beach and its swearing rainmen, one of my last two chickens died. A Silver Laced Wyandotte—black feathers sprinkled with white half-moons—she was a taciturn and gentle hen, and I made the tentative decision to bring the remaining hen, a bold and high-spirited Rhode Island Red, into the house. I had always said, as my small flock diminished, that when only one remained, it would become a house chicken and we—me and Harper, the cat and the dog—would be her flock. The cat and dog would be flock members of a carnivorous, chicken-eating variety, but flock members they would be.

The logical move would have been for me to get more chickens to keep the sole surviving hen company out in the coop, and I thought about it, I really did, but the poultry fatalities were getting to me. I hadn't minded taking care of the six-chicken flock. That part was easy. Even the winter slogs through snow and ice to let them out into their yard in the morning and to close them into their coop at night had become almost second nature, a rhythm built into my days. I was fond of the remaining chicken; I thought her preternaturally smart and dragonlike. Now she paced back and forth in the run and seemed confused and desperate. To make matters worse, in the morning I could hear her trying to *crow,* in what I was pretty sure was a forlorn attempt to attract other chickens. The muffled attempts coming from the coop sounded like a strangled rooster, but really, she wasn't half bad at it, and I was impressed beyond measure at the nobility of her efforts.

The idea of a house chicken reminded me of Paris, where I have never been, except in yet another imaginary life in which I lived there for several years, possibly even my entire life. I was inspired by my brother Jack's ex-wife Darleen, a wonderful, chaotic, and wildly funny woman who had been a model in Paris in one of her *actual* lives, and who had told me that in her apartment—I imagined a large airy space with marble floor tiles and a small balcony overlooking the rooftops of the Marais—there had lived a chicken. It seemed a cozy and warm and somehow artistic thing, both rustic and unbearably *French*, this Parisian house chicken. I had always envisioned it living in a small, clean, straw-filled wooden cage in the kitchen and spending some time walking about on the balcony every day as well. I had a certain excitement about the house chicken which harkened back to my imaginary days in Paris, the little parties in which French poets and I spouted poetry and laughed gaily about, I don't know, Proust, maybe, or cheese.

Vacated of my office, the tiny mudroom could have assumed its intended purpose as a place for muddy boots, coats, discarded shoes, wet umbrellas, firewood, mittens, and baseball caps. Instead—I'm not sure how—it turned into a Buddhist temple. It happened gradually and apparently against my will and I don't really want to go into it—the seated Buddha holding a candle, the battered little brass bowl I'd bought for a dollar at Goodwill, with its three little feet and its dented sides.

Now someone, me or the Buddha, was going to share his or her room with a chicken. My room was bigger than Buddha's and he was a nicer person. So the chicken came in and I was its roommate. We lasted a day. I don't know how they did it in Paris, but in Six Mile Beach a house chicken was not romantic, and while it did not smell as badly as you might imagine, the house quickly took on a musty, barnlike odor. Buddha and I were off the hook, and the chicken returned, gratefully, it seemed, to her coop.

But it was not lost on me, the juxtaposition between New York and Paris and Six Mile Beach. The house chicken had not been Parisian after all. The New York literary life had not interested me. Hipper-than-Me was, possibly, too hip for me. Six Mile Beach, with its restraining orders and its caféless streets, was home. I had no men at cafés, no men at all, except for two old boyfriends, a werewolf, and an imaginary date with bad hair and weird children. Life was good.

Other Forms of Leaving

So I resumed life as a cottage dweller and beach walker, the chicken went back outside, and Harper continued at school. She learned nothing (academically), saw and heard things she had never in her life even imagined (socially), made lists of words used only by the denizens of Six Mile High School, and, in what was for her an unusual move, joined the rowing team, a mixed bunch of hooligans. There are no slender and elegant crew shells involved in the rowing that goes on in Six Mile Beach. The town has a fabled lifesaving history and the high school team rows heavy, wooden, oceangoing dories: the old lifesaving boats. This had the effect of winnowing the rowing team down in rapid order. Many started and almost as many dropped out until a core of mismatched personalities and lifestyles remained. But in good weather and bad, this motley crew had one thing in common: they hauled heavy boats through high water. And an unlikely kinship was born.

She also began to drive.

For years we drive our children places. We pick them up. We feed and bathe and comfort them. We tuck them in. We pick up their crayons, boots, hair ties, dirty socks, and stray pencils. We come to chafe at some of those things. And then, suddenly, we realize that we aren't doing them anymore. Suddenly, without our even noticing it, we have bathed them for the last time, carried them on our hip for the last time. Without our even noticing it, that part is over.

You think of college as the big thing, the moment when they leave you. But it doesn't begin then. It begins with all the little steps they take away from you the second they start to walk. It begins the day they ask you not to hug them quite so much, or the day they get up by setting their own alarm. But you really believe it when they learn to drive. Then one day, she asks you if she can drive one house down to the circle at the end of the road by herself, and you let her. It's one house down. You can see her. It takes about sixty seconds. But something about seeing her head back toward you, alone behind the wheel of your car, catapults you twenty years into the future, and you suddenly know how your mother feels when she sees you, a grown woman, turning in to her driveway.

It's freedom we are talking about here. The day Aurora, Harper's friend from her Montessori days, got her license and showed up in the driveway beeping the horn on her RAV4, the two of them drove around Six Mile Beach for hours. Aurora now became, for some reason unclear to me, *Catman,* and the RAV4 became the *Catmobile.* An immediate history built up around the Catmobile, including its lack of locking doors, the alarm that went off every time said doors were opened, and the dents in the side where a jealous friend of her sister's took to the car with a baseball bat. But the main thing was, off they went, myth building.

All of these little leave-takings are supposed to get you ready for the big one, but I suspect they do not. As with the pacifier, I know it is not the same for everyone. Catman's mother had been through this with two children already, and that first day at our house with the RAV4, Catman said that she had thought her mother would cry for a couple of days after she got her license. "I was expecting it," she said. "And I admit I was a little bit insulted when all she did was text message me at two o'clock, which was the time she would normally be picking me up from school."

"Sitting in the mall," the text message read, "eating Mexican pizza."

I, on the other hand, required all kinds of hand-holding. Harper was mostly gracious when I repeatedly asked her to call me every time she got somewhere safely from somewhere else. Once, a friend of hers took her for a ride in his father's ancient Triumph. This was a car in which one could sit, hang one's hand out the window, and touch the ground with one's fingertips. The steering wheel looked like a Frisbee on a plastic stalk.

"This is my only child you have in your car," I told the boy who was driving, and spent the next half hour convinced that I had just sent my child off to her certain death. I forced myself to wait fifteen minutes before calling. She didn't even say hello. "I'm fine," she said. "Everything's fine."

She humored me. She was kind about it. When she and her friend took the ferry from the end of Six Mile Beach into Boston for an art contest interview, I offered to drive her. I text messaged her with the address and the subway stop for the school. I called her a few times but she did not pick up until after six o'clock.

"We're having dinner," she said. "I'm fine."

And she was. It took time, but I began to relax. Beneath my daughter's edgy surface was a person with a level head and a sober, observant mind. She was good and noble and honorable. Harper, in spite of our many similarities, was not the troublemaker I had been in my youth. She deserved whatever trust I could give her.

The summer after the Italian boy and the philosophy camp, the opportunity arose for her to spend six weeks at a residential precollege summer program at the Rhode Island School of Design, and I said yes, because there was nothing else I could, in good conscience, say. She was an artist. She knew the school well. She'd been taking summer courses there for years. It was only an hour away. She deserved to be able to go. She was sixteen, for God's sake. And, as was typical, there were those who thought me crazy for letting her.

Soon after her application was accepted, Harper, Thomas, and I sat in the high reaches of the RISD auditorium with about six hundred other parents and their teenagers, attending the summer program preview.

"Have these conversations with your child *before* they get here," said the Director of Resident Life. "We are not here to teach them about safe sex." He said it drolly, and everyone laughed, but I could see the mental checklists forming in the minds of hundreds of parents. Sex. *Check.* Alcohol. *Check.* Curfew. *Check.*

We'd been having the alcohol, drug, and sex conversations for years. I come from a family that is stuffed with problem drinkers, drunks, and full-out alcoholics, some sober, some still doing research. I myself had not had a drink in twenty-five years. It hadn't been hard for me to stop, and I wasn't sure I'd been an alcoholic, but I was pretty sure that if I started drinking again it would only take me about a week to get fully up to speed for the slippery slope downhill.

So Harper was informed, to put it mildly, in that regard, and in fact, had no desire to drink. These days, when you are sixteen and don't drink or do drugs, your social options are quite seriously curtailed. Especially in Six Mile Beach, where many, if not most, teenagers drank binge-fashion on a weekly basis and where, at one recent and memorable party, a full tenth of the high school student body was arrested for underage drinking. It would have been more if not for the ones who went out of the windows and hid under the house. So I admired her resolve. And although I considered myself lucky, I had recently realized that though she didn't want to drink, I'd never mentioned *how* to drink responsibly. I had to ask for help with this, since I hadn't ever drunk responsibly myself, but Jack and I came up with a pretty good set of guidelines.

Alcohol. *Check.*

Like the alcohol conversation, we'd been talking about sex since she was five or so. In this day and age, when sexual innuendo oozes from every television, radio, and magazine, many of my friends regularly bemoaned the sexualization of popular culture. Myself, I considered it a blessing to be provided with so many teaching moments.

Sex. *Check.*

.

After the RISD preview, we took a walking tour of the campus. We visited the drawing studios (easel after easel in huge, high-ceilinged, light-filled rooms) and the design studios (incomprehensible yet intrinsically beautiful three-dimensional *things*) and the nature lab (every possible kind of skeleton, egg, bone, feather, skin, fur, and claw). We visited the new library, a stunning and gorgeous revelation of modern design, unlike the *old* RISD library, which had resembled the lobby of a skid row hotel, and had not seemed to contain any books.

The day was coming. I could see it now. A little trial, a test of my ability to see what would happen when I lived alone for a while. About Harper I had no doubts. She was, to put it mildly, more than ready to be away.

My friend John said that when he walked down the street of a university town with his nineteen-year-old son, he knew what it felt like to be invisible. And indeed I could see, on this tour, two tiers of reality. The reality of us parents, fashionable or frumpy, who were there to hesitantly usher our children toward something new, and the reality of our children, who needed no ushering, and who strode down the streets of Providence, lit from within.

Returned to What

nd as I watched her walk, I thought of my youth in Cambridge and the many other places I had lived, and things I had done, real or imagined. Because Paris and New York were not my only imaginary lives. I had a way of inventing experiences for myself, and for a while it became a habit with me to recount my imaginary pasts in what I assumed was a wry and sardonic voice. I always thought people would know I was kidding, but I once convinced Harper and Thomas that I had been the Northeast Regional paintball champion and that I had gone to high school with Karl Lagerfeld. This was mystifying, because, believe me, I don't look like the ex–paintball champion of the Northeast or any of the other things I have claimed to be.

In the small town in which I grew up, in addition to the big stone church, we had a small school and a blue, blue river. My best friend in that school was a girl named Jessica David and for years we did everything together: Girl

Scouts, sleepovers, summers at the beach. Then we hit high school and she became an honor student, National Merit Scholar, and first clarinet in the school band, and I became a wastrel. She went to the finest colleges and graduate schools and when she finished, it was widely held that she went to work for the CIA, a rumor I still hold as the truth, while I smoked a lot of pot and wrote poetry. The closest I got to the CIA was at a party at the home of one of my daughter's schoolmates, where I stood beside a very large swimming pool and listened as one of the other mothers told me that her family had never known, until he retired, that her father had been in the CIA.

Not knowing that her father was attending the party and was, in fact, standing across the table from me, I said, and I was pretty sure I said it drolly, "I was in the CIA once."

The elderly man walked around the table and—in what I mistook for deadpan humor—solemnly shook my hand. I thought he was playing along. I later learned that he was senile. But I didn't know it at the time, and when he asked me where I had been stationed, I said, "Africa."

"Did you know Jim X?" he asked, and I realized, much to my horror, that he didn't know I was kidding.

I said that I didn't know Jim, and politely weaned the conversation to safer topics, ones that did not involve spouting falsehoods to noble old men. Then I excused myself and went off to visit the food tent. I apologized profusely to his daughter, who was very kind about it, and soon thereafter Harper forced me to stop making things up, and I complied, although I once came extremely close to convincing her with a single incautious comment that I was the daughter of a Romani gypsy.

I didn't recommend the wastrel life to my daughter or anyone else's daughter or to Jessica David, for that matter, but I had a hard time giving up the imaginary lives, the lives of spies, paintball champions, and gypsies. I was neither dangerous nor urbane, and did not have interesting parties. I had no BlackBerry and did not need one. I was a single mother, a beach dweller and home owner, and sometimes it all felt too much for me, the chores, the word *snow* in the forecast, the peeling paint on the bathroom ceiling. New York and Paris just seemed easier than that.

Now, for the first time in twenty years, I faced a crossroads where anything might be possible—anything—and I found that I had no idea what I wanted to be returned to, or where I wanted to go. I remembered an event I once went to, called Water Fire, in which braziers of wood burned in the canals of Providence, and gondolas glided silently among them. I longed to sit again on the edge of the canal with my fierce and infinite selves and breathe the pungent smoke for as long as I wanted. For years, maybe, if that's what it took for me to understand myself again.

And it might, I thought, take that long, and it was, I thought, all right if it did. In the meantime I would walk and wait and watch the endless variations of waves and sand, in Six Mile Beach, where once, on a day of big surf and clear water, I could see—right through the crests of the breaking combers—hundreds of small black stones held suspended in the tall waves of pale blue-green water.

Part Three

❧

Barefoot in Japan

Week One: Radical Suburbia

arper's departure for Providence was preceded by a frenzy of packing and repacking. She was organized and so was I. Organization is something I do well. I bought everything on the list. I bought a telephone and a desk lamp, neither of which she would end up using. We packed the small coffeepot. I made a large monetary deposit to the campus art supply store. She *would* use that, and then some.

On June twenty-sixth Harper, Thomas, and I drove the hour to Providence and got lost in the one-way streets surrounding the dorm. A very long line of cars snaked around three streets waiting to deposit students and luggage. We kept making wrong turns, but on our third time around the circle a kind soul let us cut, and we finally found ourselves at the staging area for arriving students.

We carried at least fifteen bags, boxes, and baskets up to her fifth-floor room, which was, I noted, *nothing* like the dorm room we had been shown on the tour. Harper did not care, I could tell. My hands itched with the desire to decorate it, or at the very least, organize it. She let me put one sheet on her bed. She let us take her out to lunch. Then she booted us out.

I breathed. Deep cleansing breaths.

And thus I commenced my new life. I don't know what I thought. She would only be gone for six weeks. It seemed like a long time, a lifetime in which to do, I don't know, everything. Lose weight, get a boyfriend, have a party. I thought my life would take on a spare simplicity much like yet another imaginary life I'd once had, that of a Japanese monk in the Honenin Temple. That I would wake in the mornings to a home that was orderly and calm. That there would be a serenity born of tidiness. Instead I sank into a slovenliness the likes of which I had never known.

I am a person who thrives on those movies and books in which the heroine—it's almost always a woman, though sometimes, as in *The Station Agent*, it is a male dwarf— suddenly finds herself in circumstances that require the restoring to order of a pigsty. My fingers start to sweat with anticipation when the heroine shows up, usually in the middle of the night, at a spider-ridden hovel. I am similarly drawn to the other version of this fairy tale, the one in which an alcoholic recluse has been living one step short of condemnation by the health department. Liquor bottles, empty take-out boxes, and dirty dishes of moldy food litter every surface. Then the alcoholic recluse sobers up and he, or the heroine or the dwarf, gets to *clean it up*, gets to wash the mildewed curtains and throw away old pizza boxes and empty bottles of scotch. In the morning he wakes to find that the hovel is situated in the midst of an orange grove, or the apartment is above a bodega whose kindly East Indian owners will become his second family and feed him lamb vindaloo and pappadam.

Now, however, seemingly inspired by the chaotic leftovers of Harper's departure, my first act as a mom-on-her-own was to become a slob. In the midst of left-behind clothing, the rope used to tie up the bedroll, Harper's unwanted bottles of moisturizer and sunscreen past its expiration date, all scattered on the living room floor during the packing process, I decided not to pick it all up and put it away—but to do nothing. Within a day or two—you would be surprised, perhaps, at how quickly it can happen—my house was movieworthy, and not in the good way.

I had new respect for the preheroine slob owners of the shack in the orange grove or the apartment above the bodega. It really only takes a day or two of not washing dishes before things become bad. I know that there are people—nice, good people—who are able to live with much more dirt than I, and I think it is a slightly healthy quality, one I usually lack due to a small germ phobia. My current state of disarray was notable for its contrast to my usual propensity for order.

When Harper was in fourth grade I became somewhat obsessed with a family I will call the Smiths. The Smiths lived in a large and gorgeous white stucco house perched on a cliff in Six Mile Beach, a house with which a great deal of care had obviously been taken. The rooms were spacious and light filled; the windows were huge and plentiful and interestingly shaped and framed views of the ever-changing sea. The kitchen was a chef's dream, and the house was stuffed with intriguing artwork, handmade furniture, cutting-edge electronics, and expensive musical instruments. The members of this family all spoke fluent French though they were not French, and they actually *played* those musical instruments at a highly proficient level. In spite of this, they appeared to be completely immune to serious dirt.

The first time I arrived at their house to pick up Harper after a sleepover, I walked with her into the kitchen and was stunned into immobility by a sight I'd never actually seen in real life. Every surface was covered with dishes and pots and pans on which dried, days-old food remained. Three additional piles of dishes and pans teetered by the sink. The dishwasher was running. On the counter, among the mail and empty wine glasses, were the gluey, unwashed bowl in which the previous day's cookies had been mixed and the crusted string that had tied the dinner roast together. The mother walked in behind me, gestured nonchalantly, and said something like, "I got behind."

On another day, three large green trash bags had been ripped open in the entryway. Garbage—and this was food, not paper—was strewn around the foyer. Two small dogs foraged through the piles. When the mother came out to greet me, I gestured nervously toward the floor, but she just kept chatting. The Smiths really *did* need a heroine.

I am not saying that I had trash on my floor. But there were mornings when I got up to find the counters and sink stacked with dirty dishes and pans. There were days when I didn't clean them up right away, sometimes not until they had grown with the addition of breakfast and lunch leftovers. I never in a million years would have allowed this to happen when Harper was home. I didn't know why it was happening now. It might have been a simple act of rebellion against the dailiness of picking up after someone else. It might have been an expression of grief, but it felt too satisfying for that. I might have been doing it just because I could.

Along with sinking into sloth, I began a relentless and seemingly futile attempt to rearrange the living room furniture, something I did so often that a goal of mine was to live in a house in which all of the furniture was bolted to the floor.

I moved the living room bookcases to my office. Books were strewn all over the floor and on the kitchen table. I read once in a newspaper that when you spiff up your house, you should clear from your rooms everything that is smaller than a basketball, and so I began to view every little bit of décor with that in mind. A moot point since there essentially was no décor left, only a clump of furniture in the middle of the living room, and no order whatsoever.

But the curtains billowed in the cold June breezes of Six Mile Beach, and I now had time, in the midst of my self-induced chaos, to watch them billow for hours. I wondered if I was going to spend the whole summer redecorating my living room, staring out windows, and living in squalor. Was I going to squander my precious self-discovery time on décor? For a while it looked as if I might.

Unlike the previous summer, when my time alone had been purposeful and focused, this time was chaotic and formless. That time had felt like a "break." This time felt like practice for a newly visible future. I knew that the day was coming when Harper would be gone for far more than two weeks or six. And even though this *was* a trial run in many ways—the dorms and the roommate and the classes and the independence and me alone in a very dirty house—it was still only a trial, and the ability to fall apart felt a little like fun, rather than a premonition of formlessness to come.

Week Two: A Few More Things About My Mother and Me

As I puttered around my newly messy house in a combined state of shock and freedom, I thought of the other houses I had loved—farmhouses and garden sheds and garrets overlooking the church that Emily Dickinson attended and then didn't attend when she dressed in white and never went out and stitched her poems together with sewing needles. This love of place I got from my mother, whose house, in stark contrast to my own small and newly postapocalyptic one, was large and, not surprisingly, well kept. She had moved there almost thirty years before and she had quickly wrestled the brand-new house and barren yard into submission. Now it resembled a small farm, with an orchard, birdhouses that birds actually lived in, and a cadre of hummingbirds that dive-bombed and chased each other around the yard chattering angrily in their fierce territorial battles.

It was my mother's house, safe and clean, that saved

me right before my separation, when I knew it was coming but it hadn't quite arrived. I had entertained a notion that I would move back to Connecticut and set up household in the bosom of my family, and so I sat at my mother's kitchen table and looked through the real estate section of the *PennySaver*. She didn't know about the coming separation, but never asked me why I went to look at houses. One house sailed like a Chinese boat in the woods near the home I grew up in. Another had a tiny tower and a family of swans, their awkward gaits, their bowing for crumbs. My mother's house and these others made me understand that although my life felt a little bit over, I had other rooms left in me.

It was in the house of my childhood that I rearranged furniture for the first time. I was twelve and I wanted to push the antique bed that had been in my father's family for generations into an alcove under the eaves. It would have fit perfectly were it not for the exceptionally tall bedposts. My mother and her friend Lily were having coffee in the kitchen. When I told them about the bed, my mother went directly to the garage, Lily and I trailing in her wake, and got a saw. She then went upstairs and sawed the bedposts entirely off, while I watched in horrified admiration and Lily just watched in horror.

"Have you lost your mind?" Lily asked.

My mother looked at us with grim satisfaction.

I hold this memory close to my heart, along with the red lipstick, the praying, the wand, and the chasing my brother around the garden with a broom. My mother was still the woman I feared and admired most, and her house was the house in which I felt the safest. And once, when my daughter needed a place to hang her art portfolio, I didn't think twice before hammering a large nail into some pretty nice bookcases.

Harper's leaving was a lesson in letting go, and in the natural order of things—life and age and change. I was learning by watching my mother that aging happens in plateaus. It happens in almost imperceptible increments, but increments just the same. And stubborn and strong as she was, my mother was getting older. I noticed it whenever I saw her. Her voice was a little bit softer, and sometimes she slept for a few minutes in the afternoon when she sat in her leather chair to sew. She was smart and clever, and read books even I would not tackle, but due to hearing-aid malfunctions, our conversations sometimes took excessively odd turns.

Me: Mom, do you have the recipe for the oatmeal

cookies you used to make when we were kids?

Mom: I have a lot of good oatmeal cookie recipes.

Me: But you know the ones you made when we were kids?

Mom: I have a recipe for icebox cookies. You put them in the freezer and cut off what you need.

Me: But are they oatmeal cookies? The ones you made when we were kids? It's the oatmeal cookies I'm looking for. Are the icebox cookies those?

Mom: I guess so. Have you read *Love in the Time of Cholera*?

Me: No. Was it good? Don't give away the end.

Mom: I won't, but when you get to the end, I just want to let you know that I am fermenting.

Me: *What?*

Mom: Can't say, because it would be giving away the end.

Me: Okay.

Mom: Who was that guy whose kids went to school with Harper?

Me: Which guy?

Mom: The guy in a band.

Me: That was Steve Tyler.

Mom: Was it Bono?

Me: No, it was Steve Tyler.

Mom: Who?

Me: Steve Tyler.

Mom: Not Bono.

Me: No.

Mom: Because I saw something on TV about Bono, and I wondered.

Me: No, it's a different guy.

Mom: Okay.

I could relate to this conversational mayhem because I saw it happening between Harper and me. Sometimes I asked Harper a question she had just answered fifteen minutes before. And more often than I liked to admit, she'd ask, "What did you say?" and I would have to answer, "I was talking to the dog," or worse, "I was muttering." I could see she thought I'd lost a step or two in the verbal department, though she admired my creativity and the fact that, as I liked to remind her, I could still pick her up.

My mother once told me that she knew that she and I had not had the bond that Harper and I had. She was right, but we had made do. Sometimes, when I reflected on the course our relationship had taken, on the differences between my mother and me, I tried to remember all of the similarities and the things she had given us. Jack once said to me that he appreciated that my mother had encouraged our creativity. And it was true that all three of us were, in one way or another, makers of things, builders of boats or boxes or books.

"I don't remember her doing that," I said.

"You don't?"

"No. I just remember her never saying anything about it. A kind of benign neglect."

"That's what I mean," he said.

And it was true that my mother had let us run where we wanted. My childhood was a pastiche of happy, seemingly adult-free days bound by the river, stone walls, meadows, and woods, by the wind in the sycamores, the worn red leather chair in our living room, the screen door with its dangling hook, by the warm rocks, the dust in the dirt road, soft as powder, and the Milky Ways of fireflies above the river meadows soaked in mist. We spent our days on the river and on my grandparents' farm, where we explored the brook that wended its way through boulders and cedar trees, and where I steadfastly remember riding on the back of a bull named Duncraggen. In those days we were all going to live as children forever, throwing sticks high into the air at twilight, chanting incantations. We were going to stand for eternity at the base of the waterfall, between a tall stone outcrop and the pouring water, holding a large fishnet and filling it again and again with the spawning buckeyes that poured over the fall like water itself.

My mother was going to live forever, too, with her black hair and her cotton dresses, looking up to show Andrew and me a bald eagle flying overhead. Now, of course, I saw that she was not immortal. Each time I left her house, and saw her waving to me from her driveway as I turned to go down the hill, I thought to myself that it might be the last time I ever saw her. *There should be a law*, I told Jack, *that mothers have to live forever.*

Week Three: Around Providence

So my mother was power-washing, I was doing nothing, and I had no idea what Harper was doing. The dorms had a curfew and it was strictly enforced. She had classes all day and a lot of homework. Otherwise, she could do whatever she wanted. I really wasn't very worried about what she would do. What got to me was that I didn't know. I couldn't ask her my litany of annoying, glare-inducing questions about where she was going and who she would be with, were any of them pot smokers, who was driving, how long had they been driving, were they a *good* driver, did they drink. I couldn't tell her to please be careful in certain parts of town, better yet don't go there at all, are you sure you want to wear that outfit, do you know where the emergency phones are located, and is your cell phone charged. I was sure she was thrilled.

❧

On her first weekend she came home for a day, to get some forgotten miscellanea, and uploaded her photos onto the computer to give me a slide show. One picture came up—a dark space I couldn't quite make out.

"Oh," she said. "I forgot to tell you. We went to a hookah bar." I knew they existed, dim rooms in which you sat on the floor and smoked flavored tobacco from hookahs.

"You don't inhale," she said.

Yeah, yeah, I thought.

I told a couple of friends. They were a little bit aghast, as if it had been *opium*. They couldn't understand why I wasn't upset.

The second week, I drove down to meet her for lunch. When we'd talked the night before, she said, "Oh, there's something I should tell you before you come."

"You didn't get a tattoo," I said.

"No."

"You didn't bleach your hair."

"I gauged my ears."

Ear gauging is the process of expanding pierced earlobes and I associate it with the memory of a guy who worked in the food co-op we went to when Harper was a toddler; his face was riddled with safety pins and his ears sported holes the size of pencil erasers. Little did I know that eraser-sized holes were *nothing.*

"How big?" I asked.

"Not very big," she said. "They look really good."

I have an aversion to body modification for teenagers. Mostly I just don't like the way it usually looks, and I worry about irreversibility. But I have to say, the ears didn't look bad. They looked kind of cool. I googled ear gauging. Everyone agreed. They shrink back.

We talked frequently, and intensive text messaging became part of my life once again. Because I didn't want to call her every day, I did the best I could with the texting, but I confess that I expected too much. I expected lengthy conversations, long messages back and forth, but on the other side of the cell tower, my correspondent was less interested than I was. I would later learn how busy she was and how hot and how tired. "I fall asleep drawing," she would tell me later, "and wake up hours later, still dressed, in a puddle of drool."

When I visited her, we walked through the overhot streets to an Indian store where the proprietor gave us glass rings and other little favors from a straw basket by the door. Everything jingled and shone. They had Indian bedspreads of the kind I had used when I was eighteen. I was glad to see them again, glad to know that they still existed and that young women bought them and draped them on their beds or hung them up for curtains. We bought earrings for Harper and little belled camels on a beaded string for me. It was so good to see her, and hard to leave.

The next day, I went with Sage to the Hopper retrospective at Boston's Museum of Fine Arts, where small mobs vied for position in front of lighthouses and diners. I'm not fond of museums and their crowds but I like paintings just fine, and I *love* brushstrokes. I like to see how what appears to be perfect from afar becomes, at close range, mortal.

I moved through Hopper's buildings and windows and lighthouses and the diners with their sad-looking patrons. But it was the last painting that stalled me in my tracks for a good long time. *Sun,* it was called, *in an Empty Room.* I understood that room, and the longing for it and the fear of it. I understood the sunlight. I understood both sides of the empty. In that room, I thought, much had already happened. In that room, anything could happen now.

Afterward, we had lunch in the café, and I bought

some postcards in the shop, and put them in the pile of things I was sending to Harper, something every few days, a postcard with a cryptic message or a box with some stones from the beach, a clipping from the police log, a Starbucks card.

Week Four: My Brother's Wedding

Smack in the middle of our six-week experiment with separation, my brother Andrew got married. He was fifty-eight; Laura, his bride, was fifty-six and starry-eyed, though both had been married before. I was six years divorced and not a positive thinker. They say that love and poetry require a willing suspension of disbelief but, let's face it, the love metaphors aren't promising. We're in over our heads, jumping off the deep end, head over heels, out of our minds, moths to flames, spellbound, hearts on fire, falling hard. Now, single, in the middle of life, not only could I not suspend disbelief, I was positively wedded to it. There are too many things on earth that I do not understand about marriage. It starts so hopefully, and we go into it so willingly, like lambs. I was jaded. But Andrew and Laura were not. They were willing to suspend disbelief.

❧

In the realm of marriage, I am a survivor, a refugee, an itinerant wanderer, and I have a bad habit of collecting jaded marriage quotes:

A good husband is hard-working and absent.

The ingredients of a good marriage are courtesy and great sex.

I was eighteen. It was my first penis, and I married it. What a mistake.

This made shopping for a wedding card treacherous. My first stop, at a high-end card shop in Richer-than-Me, showed promise when a woman standing next to me in front of the wedding cards leaned over and said, "Isn't this cute?" and showed me a card that, when opened, played Israel Kamakawiwoʻole singing "Somewhere over the Rainbow." I came of age in the sixties and Harper has high musical expectations of me. That I liked Israel Kamakawiwoʻole singing "Somewhere over the Rainbow" would fill her with stunned disbelief.

The woman wondered aloud who the singer was, and I told her. "Where did you find it?" I asked.

"Here," she said, pointing, "but, sorry, I'm taking the last two," and walked away.

"I would have given one to *her*," I complained to Jack

later as we commiserated about the impossibility of finding good wedding cards. He was not sympathetic.

"You don't have a leg to stand on," he said, which was what he always said.

My next stop was a chain drugstore. There I found a wide variety of terribly sappy wedding cards and a very large number of musical cards, which seem to be highly in vogue at the moment. The only one I liked played "The Chicken Dance" when I opened it, but I knew I needed something more heartfelt than that.

My third stop was the local bookstore where I had stumbled through my first book reading and signing, somehow managing to compare my memoir with a Bengal tiger. How that happened I do not know. But there I found a lovely watercolor card of two geese flying, under which was printed a Native American wedding blessing that was perfect save for the part that said "May we become one person, with one breath." I couldn't spring for it (codependent no more and all that) but I finally settled on a card that was pretty on the outside and wished happiness on the inside, briefly and simply, and with sincerity I truly felt.

The wedding day dawned clear and sunny. I picked up Harper in Providence on the way south to the Connecticut shore. Halfway through her residence, she looked pale and felt hot and miserable. If I had known she was about to topple into two weeks of bronchitis, I wouldn't have made her go to the wedding, but I didn't know and she soldiered on.

The wedding took place on the bank of a river, on a stone patio under a white canopy. Jack's girlfriend, Anne, tall and elegant, wore a black dress and a hat. I wore black pants and, in homage to the thus far elusive Japan, an off-white kimono jacket. I walked with the ailing Harper across the long wide lawn to the river. The lawn was dry and hot, as was her forehead. The stones of the patio were uneven, the chairs and tables wobbly.

Laura walked across the terrace to the recorded strains of a song she had written herself when she first met Andrew. Jack was as wedding-phobic as I was, and we had worried about the song, not knowing what it would be like and fearing sentimentality. I would tell him afterward that I had choked on a carrot right before the song started to play, which was true. But the real reason my eyes filled with tears was not because of the song, which was lovely, or because of the bride, walking down the aisle with a truly happy smile on her face. I teared up because Andrew, the noble and quiet man who had endured a very bitter divorce after a very long marriage, the weathered man with a wide, well-defended heart and few words, stood alone in front of the wedding guests with tears in his eyes. The sight of him filled me with a massive and protective love I had not expected to feel. The deep bond of our childhood kicked in: a time when I had adored him and had been his constant companion and cohort in adventures of field and river. I cried for his willingness, and for his vulnerability. I cried because he was up there alone, with his heart wide open.

Before the toast a waiter dropped a tray of mimosas onto the gray stone tiles of the patio. The eating of the cake inexplicably involved the singing of "Old MacDonald." One fellow, quite drunk, cut loose with some serious dance moves. A baby cried. But it was the song that stayed with me. Everyone got a CD as a wedding favor and for days afterward I played it. I played it *a lot*. Once, when I drove the hour to meet Harper for lunch, I played it the entire way there and all the way home. I never mentioned it to her, because if she thought the Israel Kamakawiwoʻole version of "Somewhere over the Rainbow" was sappy, she would have never let me live down the wedding song. The hair on my arms rose every time I played it.

I didn't understand my brother or his bride. I didn't

understand their courage. I thought of Hunter, who still e-mailed me—"I love you," and "Are you there?"—and I thought of Harold, married all these years, since we had called it quits—and I wondered with what sort of man I would be willing to abandon myself, however briefly, however fleetingly, however blindly. For whom I would suspend disbelief, fall head over heels, risk the werewolf to get the guy.

Week Five: Philosopher Kings: Romeo, Romeo

Quite a few people I knew had met through the Internet, and so, after the wedding, still in the midst of sloth, emboldened by renewed relationships with Hunter and Harold, spurred on by envy or curiosity, and in a willful disregard of my nature, I decided to check out the hipper of the two main Internet dating services, the one that requires you to fill out an extensive personality profile and has the word *harmony* in its name. A few years earlier, I had checked out the other service, the one with *dot* in its name, on which people give themselves screen names such as JohnfromHarvard, SailboatBill, LookingforLove, and AGoodMan. But after encountering BoxersorBriefs, TheKindBull, and BigJim, who described himself, astonishingly, as a big guy who liked big hooters, I bailed out.

I filled out the questionnaire—this took *hours*—and the service began to send me matches. Immediately I suspected that something was wrong. First, I got very few matches. In his short time with the service, one friend had gotten tons of matches, and good ones. He had sent me his lists. *Artist, teacher, therapist, coach.* My lists worried me: *heavy equipment operator, janitor, taxidermist.*

Harper once told me cheerfully that over 50 percent of the people on online dating services are lying about something. They lie about age, weight, marital status, income, and, according to something she read in *Vogue*, gender.

"Gender?" I asked, incredulous.

"That's what I read," said she. "Sexual preference, too."

Still, I browsed. The applicants quickly started to sound the same. They liked the same things and wanted the same things. They wanted romantic suppers and sunset walks on the beach. They wanted a strong emotional relationship, "LTR," and marriage. They sounded a little whiny, and it was possible that they were all versions of the same man. But in spite of my bad attitude, I found a retired, vegetarian, Buddhist candidate who sounded interesting and looked okay. Actually, he looked like a cross between Richard Dreyfuss and Kris Kringle, but he wasn't a taxidermist, so I wrote to him anyway.

Dear X,

Here are a few brief notes about me and my life. I live in a small house near the ocean with my daughter (age

16), my dog, our cat, and one chicken. I grew up in Connecticut, on the river. I have two brothers, one older, one younger, both of whom still live there. My mother lives there as well. She is 83 and frighteningly spry.

I am typically a calm, contemplative sort.[1] I'm very content being alone, a habit that may be hard to break, and frankly it's possible that I will end up not wanting to. But I've reached the point where I'm thinking it might be something to explore.

My dog is 5 years old. My cat is 12. My chicken is 4.

That's about it for now. Thanks for writing. I hope you write again.

Sincerely,
Catherine

It was easier to write this summary than I imagined it would have been to say it in person. One of the things that had appealed to me about Hunter was the idea that with him, I would not have to tell my story from scratch.

---

[1] True about the contemplative, not about the calm.

How dreary, I thought, to sit over coffee after coffee with new candidates and recite the details of my life over and over, while simultaneously evaluating attraction quotients and pheromone levels, second-guessing wardrobe choices, and deciding if I liked the sound of someone's voice. When you are young and going through these motions, you have less life to report, fewer failures, and you probably care less about clothing. At least, *I* had cared less about clothing. I had been more centered. I had doubted myself less. When I told my story then, I really liked it. Now, it was not so simple.

X was slightly briefer, but definitely more businesslike about the summary of his past. He got it over with, lickety-split: the long marriage, the recent divorce, the subsequent relationship with a brilliant Ivy League professor. My hackles went up a bit at that, as they did with his references to Proust and Mozart. I was forced to take intelligent—yet poetic—countermeasures.

So I countered with Proust and the far more interesting—I thought—Melville. I ignored the Mozart. Classical music was all right, and I was completely in love with the Bach cello solos, but my musical tastes had become strongly influenced by Harper, who owned a record player, was partial to "vinyl," and listened to everyone from early, Sid Barrett–era Pink Floyd to the brilliant and short-lived Television to Frankie Valli's "Walk Like a

Man" to sixties music even I, who had grown up then, had
never heard of. My current favorite song was the Flaming
Lips' symphonic, postapocalyptic, dirgelike "Gash." I decided not to mention music.

Dear X,

Proust falls into the same category as Melville.
Writes a great sentence, a great paragraph, goes on
for too long. I read Moby Dick regularly, one paragraph at a time, selected at random. I've read the
whole thing in order. I know the story. And as for
Proust, do you know that gossip increases the pro-
duction of endorphins? Maybe this is why he was in
bed for so long.

You should be aware that having worked hard as a
reader in my younger years, and as a writer all my
life, I am now an equal opportunity reader and do not
like to work hard for books. I recommend the Moom-
introll books, which are, in my controversial opinion,
better than Winnie the Pooh.

Please also keep in mind that I am wary and suspi-
cious and part of me would like not to do this at all.
Those are the facts. A cup of tea, I can do. A cup of
tea tells it all. You have one. Then you know if you

want to have a salad. I can do e-mails. I can do tea.[2]
Having never done this before, is that what people do?
Meet for lunch? Coffee? Tea? Scotch?[3]

That's funny about the rooster. My brother once had
his own DNA analyzed. A guy I grew up with was a
friend of Andy Warhol's.[4]

Catherine

Although I intended to be completely myself in this
e-mail relationship, I could see that an alter ego seemed
to be taking over already.

Dear X,

My day so far: Printing a picture of my daughter's face
reflected in the tea kettle. Letting the chicken out.
Bribing my dog with a piece of bread. Later today I
am going to see a Unitarian minister who on one of
my few visits to his church, years ago, sang part of "By
the River of Babylon" during his sermon. He sang it

---

[2] This would turn out to be a lie.

[3] Just kidding on the scotch.

[4] He was the crotch model for the Rolling Stones album *Sticky Fingers*,
but I didn't go into that.

quietly. A few people quietly joined in. Once I told him that I didn't believe in God, and he said, "Which God don't you believe in?" Anyone who says that, I will follow to the moon.

My brother found out that he is 11% Asian. Which I attribute to the proximity of Asia to Eastern Europe (45%) rather than the 40 or so % Western European. (I hope this adds up to 100% or he is either part bionic or missing something.) I'm assuming my DNA would have similar percentages, but apparently siblings do not necessarily carry the same configurations. That said, I always knew I was Asian.

The highlights of my wilderness experience: I have seen an ermine in the wild, a fisher cat, and a stealth fighter plane.

Keep in mind that I watch movies. I watch television. I like to say that I am 75% soulful and smart and 25% pop culture. I suspect a DNA analysis would confirm this.

Catherine

About the television. I was not very discriminating about television. X had told me that he was a member of

Mensa. I was now giving him a test. Could he deal with *Project Runway*? And so, okay, could he deal with *Survivor*?

Dear X,

It has come to my attention that you have not answered my most recent e-mail. I attribute this to the television reference. I am assuming one of the following scenarios has taken place:

1. You are horrified at the thought of dating a television watcher and don't know how to say so. You wanted me to be above television watching, oh well.

2. You are spending a week watching television in order to assess my intelligence. Can you stand it? Are you in love enough with my wit and intelligence that you can forgive the TV to get the girl? I confess that I am predisposed to this scenario. If you are trying it on for size, I might still want you.[5]

3. You are immersed in Scenario One and can't decide whether you should simply "close communication" or send me an e-mail, informing me of your inabilities.

---

[5] Racking up the lies.

Please note: Elaine and Willem de Kooning read mystery novels on the train to Black Mountain College, where they once took a walk into the forest at night and stood beneath the vaulted, starry sky. Then Bill said, "Let's go back to the party. The universe gives me the creeps." Hunter watches television and reads Field and Stream. He writes with great wit. He shoots deer with a long bow. Harold listens to NPR and reads the New Yorker. I am fond of both Harold and Hunter, and of the De Koonings, too, and all of their various media.

Catherine

As I wrote the e-mails, I became less and less interested in actually meeting Kris "Not His Real Name" Kringle, who once said that he almost smashed his head on the keyboard he laughed so hard when he read my latest e-mail. This made me feel guilty that I didn't find his e-mails interesting. He billed himself as funny but he told bad jokes. Mozart and Proust notwithstanding, if you profess to be funny, you have to carry through on it. I began to long for handsome, bad men with interesting minds and motorcycles. I longed for a man with scars on his face, who may turn into a werewolf but never in front of me. I didn't want ever again to be the sailor's wife, to pack the groceries and worry about having enough soap or paper towels. I wanted to jitterbug. The kind where you get thrown around.

But X loved my e-mails. He thought they were amusing and erudite and, in fact, I agreed. I tended to be more interesting on paper than in real life, but he didn't know that. He wanted to get together. He wanted me to call him. He wanted to take me to a café. He said he thought the television bit was funny, but I didn't believe him. He used one big word every e-mail and started to give me the creeps.

My case, I felt, was complicated. I knew that a big reason I was carrying on with X, albeit at a great distance, was because Harper was away and I had time on my hands. But though she would have been delighted to see me happily ensconced in a relationship, I knew that it wasn't time for me to embark on that voyage. I had a year left with Harper at home, and I didn't want to spend it with Kris Kringle. After a while, I waited too long to answer his latest e-mail and he shut me down. This was called "closing communication." I confess that I was relieved. Jack once told me that when he first met his girlfriend and liked her a lot, he did not feel, as he expected, excitement or happiness.

"What did you feel?" I asked him.

"Despair," he said.

I was surprised to learn that many of my single friends in my age bracket found themselves in a similar boat, the boat in which one reluctantly decides to look again at men after some time of calling it quits. Scarlet and I chatted about it at a party.

"I'm not really interested, but the thought of spending the rest of my life alone is kind of, like, depressing. So I'm dating someone but I just can't get around the whole idea of it," said Scarlet.

"You mean romance?" I asked. "Or sex?"

"Both," she said.

I told her about X.

"You were writing him."

"I was."

"No desire to meet him."

"Right. It was just so hard to think about making a phone call," I said, "or giving up my number. There was this kind of dread about hearing his voice."

"What did he say about this?" asked Scarlet.

"He said, 'You do know that this is a Web site for people who are interested in dating, right?'"

"That was clever."

"It was."

"You might just be the kind of person," Jack had told me "who's going to have to meet a guy in the post office."

"Easy for you to say," I said. "Have you met any men in the post office lately?"

I repeated this comment to Scarlet.

"Only the ones in the wanted posters," she said.

I don't know what it is that creates such reluctance to take the leap again in matters of romance. At first perhaps it is weariness and later just habit, but after a while of not having made the hurdle, the course just seems daunting and, frankly, when one weighs the pros and cons of having a man in one's life after a marital failure, you tend to think that the pro list might be short. It might be limited to snow shoveling and bailing the flooded basement. But my interlude with X had provided a brief respite from my increasingly formless days, which were, finally, starting to bother me.

Week Six: Barefoot in Japan

lthough I had a Buddha in the mudroom and was convinced I had once had a shaved head and saffron robe and had lived in the Honenin Temple, and though I sometimes liked to pretend that I had an invisible Japanese chef—who prepared dumplings, miso soup, slivers of cucumber and avocado embedded in sticky rice and rolled in sesame seeds, aduki beans, and thin buckwheat pancakes spread with apple butter—of course, I did not. I lived with dust and dog hair. I lived with an unruly garden and a tendency toward entropy. I had a great deal of work to do, and I was the only monk. The work I did in this home, and the work I had done to make it, had been, in large part, to make a home for Harper. I had been propelled by that fierce mother-bear thing. Denning. Protecting. But now there were sometimes days when I was overwhelmed by the sheer number of things I needed to do for the upkeep of my cottage, and those that I could not, alone, manage. I had a handyman, whom I referred to as my surrogate husband. He was an associate monk, I guess. He did what I could not do.

One of my burdens that summer was my dog, Sam—a ruffian and scoundrel—and her hobby of ridding the world of rabbits. In spite of Sam and the multitudinous coyotes, a veritable world population of rabbits appeared at my house every summer and encircled the foundation of my house with their many nests. One might correctly imagine that when one combines a rabbit-hunting machine with a plethora of bunny nests, a great deal of mayhem ensues.

My mother, to no one's surprise, shared my dog's proclivities. Her targets were chipmunks and mice, which she caught and relocated (chipmunks), or caught and threw away (mice). In the case of the latter, I believe she froze them first, for some reason having to do with the timing of her trips to the dump.

"If I die," she said, "and you find a bag of mice in the freezer, that's why."

Baby rabbits look like baby deer, sleepy, but wild, with little folded ears, and to my mother's amusement, every summer I made one small attempt to save them by protecting one of their nests with a makeshift fence. It was futile, because they didn't stay in the nests for long. They moved very soon to the nearby bushes, where my dog could flush them out and from which they inevitably threw themselves, in a desperate attempt to save their tiny lives, into the window wells where my dog could not go. The window wells were small and they were deep and what would happen was that I would hear a thumping sound and I would find baby bunnies in there and I would have to get them out.

I had to lie facedown on the ground, *prone*, in order to reach the bottom of the window wells. In order to get to the facedown part, I had to kneel first, and my knees were old and unwell, and the ground was rough and covered with pebbles. (After the bunny fishing expeditions, my forearms and knees were studded with small pebbles, bits of turf, and dozens of tiny purple bruises.) And to make it all worse, I discovered that I was *afraid* of baby rabbits and that even though I was doing them a favor they were terrified of me as well, and though they were babies, they were not sleepy immobile babies and had a surprising amount of pep, and when I tried to catch them, they jumped around those window wells like bats. I tended to scream while I caught them and that probably didn't help. If Phoebe was around, she would help me. She didn't mind, and she wasn't afraid of them. If she heard me screaming, she'd come out. But Phoebe wasn't always home.

And as I fearfully wrangled the bunnies out of window wells, I thought longingly of my imaginary Japanese ancestors standing quietly by in their heavy trousers, their kimono silks, and the thick padded brocade jackets in which they rode into battle looking very fashionable. But in that life I suspected I would have had servants. If I had fished rabbits out of window wells, dirtying my kimono or my quilted jacket, someone would have whipped out yet another silk outfit for me, or would have caught the bunnies in my stead, and cooked them. Instead, I had Phoebe in her summer garb of baggy nylon shorts and a T-shirt, who talked gently to them and scooped them up carefully in my old leather work gloves. Occasionally I saved the inhabitants of an unearthed nest and took a little box of four-inch bunnies to the wildlife center, where I was made to fill out a form. Under "Type of Animal," I wrote "Bunnie." The clinic worker crossed it out and wrote "Cottontail."

"I knew that," I said. She didn't answer.

Though I still extricated them from the window wells, the rest of my protective measures were futile and, over time and out of necessity, I stopped paying attention to the dog and the rabbits and let nature take its toll. I slowly regained a sense of order. I resumed my walks on the seawall, where the guy with the kite was at it again. Old men sat in lawn chairs in the back of a pickup truck. Small children rediscovered the ocean. I came around. I came to. I emerged from sloth. I did laundry. I cleared off the kitchen counters and returned stacks of books to their rightful places. I put the living room back together. I holed up for three days so that I could read the final Harry Potter book without anyone telling me how it ended. My second day of reading was a cold and foggy July day in Six Mile Beach. By noon I had a sweater on and all my windows closed. I read all day and into the night and awoke the next morning relieved. I would be all right.

Then Japan finally kicked in.

I have a black book with a red ideogram stamped on the cover. The edges of the binding are frayed, but the book has a good heft: the pages are dense and solid and the cover is not stained. The book is called *The Importance of Living* by Lin Yutang. He tells the story of someone called Chin Shegt'an who was once stranded in a temple for ten days in a rainstorm and to pass the time he and his friend made a list of life's thirty-three truly happy moments.

Why thirty-three moments? I don't know. Perhaps it seemed like a pleasing number, or maybe that's all they thought of before it stopped raining. But I like to imagine that they thought of many, maybe hundreds, or even thousands, of moments of happiness and then spent the ten days paring them down and arranging them, like haiku syllables or lotus blossoms.

Chin Shegt'an's list was simple. He opened a window so a wasp could fly out. It was a clear morning after a month of rain. He accidentally broke a bowl made of fine porcelain and it broke into so many pieces that he knew it was not reparable. He held the pieces in his hands, then he gave them to a friend and said, *Never let this bowl come into my sight again.*

I understood Chin Shegt'an. He had become, over the years, one of my heroes. And as the final days of my summer alone passed, I found myself at last alone in a temple. The days were hot and dry. A water ban went into effect. Everything was quiet. No one did much, no one I knew, no one in my neighborhood, no one, it seemed, anywhere. The chicken stood on her tree stump every afternoon and looked into the distance. On the kitchen table I kept a box of small white stones. I had no appointments. I turned each calendar page and found yet another day white and radiant in its emptiness. The grass in the yard turned brown and then brittle and crunched beneath my bare feet when I walked to the garden. I felt suspended in the thin, fine air, a moment in time, a time without a story, a suspension of matter, until everything was about the rituals of the day, the precise moment in which a thing can be written, thought, or executed: the moment of awakening when I put my hand on the dog's head. The moment at night of closing the hen into her coop, doing the dishes, drying the counter, and lowering the bamboo shades. The moment of beginning and of ending when I looked around and thought: *Done.* And that was a moment of happiness.

Part Four

What Kind of Wind

The Fall of the Honenin Temple

Then my girl came home. Everything changed the minute Thomas and I started to fill my car with much more stuff than went off with her in June. Piles of paintings. Stacks of sketchbooks. A sextant. A small structure made entirely of toothpicks and glue, that could hold up the weight of a brick. Boxes and bags of art supplies paid for by the early-summer offering to the campus supply store. (When I later received the itemized receipt, the list of paint, paper, canvas, gesso, Gamsol, brushes, charcoal, wire, and binding thread was sprinkled throughout with Snickers bars and caffeine pills.) She was tired and pale and thin. She was soaked in art. She had seen the sun come up way more than once.

Six weeks is not long, and every mother knows that it takes almost the whole time one's child is away to get used to his or her absence and find a rhythm of one's own. I had discovered in the last days of the summer a particular and orderly life, a serene tidiness, and then, as the car emptied out, the film ran in reverse: the counters and floors that had been neat and orderly once again became strewn with luggage and art and clothing. I tried to stem the tide.

"Let's throw these clothes right down to the laundry," I said.

"Let's take these right upstairs."

"Let's put this shampoo and stuff right into the bathroom."

And then I surrendered to the vortex. It was easier than I thought it would be. My heart had *liked* the Honenin Temple, but it didn't live there. It was so good to have her back, this person who left black clothing in her wake.

She slept for a couple of days and then we began to renegotiate living in the same house again, my need for order, hers for independence. I could see that she was now ready for something beyond Six Mile Beach. The town was no longer big enough or full enough, and it no longer gave her much joy. And although I understood that, it broke my heart just a little. In my mind she was still seven, wearing an elf costume.

Shortly after her return, we set out for our annual vacation with thirty-five or so of our closest friends, at the worse-than-rustic former YWCA called Riverbend where Hunter and I had had our imaginary reunion. I had been going there for almost twenty-five years and Harper had gone since she was three. Riverbend was the antithesis of the temple. Suffice it to say that the first time I went, I almost turned around and left. The floors were a combination of linoleum and indoor-outdoor carpeting. The main room was furnished solely by several long folding tables and metal folding chairs. We all shared four bedrooms—no private rooms—and three bathrooms. Sagging cots and torn mattresses were the sleeping accommodations.

Attached to the rambling house was a large worn barn with a soaring ceiling and a sleeping loft. In our years at Riverbend, four generations of teenagers had populated that loft, and the children who now played in the barn were the children of young men and women who were themselves children when I first met them. A round above-ground pool was situated in the overgrown brush behind the main building. At any time of night or day, children, and adults acting like children, frolicked under the eye of a designated lifeguard.

Our ages ranged from one to seventy. Some of us were related, but most of us were not. Our children had known each other all their lives and, although most of them did not live near each other, they were bonded at the soul. If Harper had to choose between Riverbend and Christmas, she would choose Riverbend.

Riverbend was our extended, unofficial family, the one that augmented and counterbalanced our own families. A

raucous, nondrinking family that was prone to unpredict-
ability. Once Aurora came to visit and arrived during dinner. When Harper introduced her to the assembled
diners, they began chanting her name loudly.

"I hope," she said later, "that will happen again some-
time in my life." For those of us at Riverbend, such things
were commonplace, and for this reason we returned, year
after year, sagging mattresses and all.

For ten days, there were no computers and no television,
no radio. Manners and vague familial guidelines were followed. Petty grievances arose, were resolved or ignored,
and then passed. No teenager slept at night or was awake
before noon. No one did much, and not much happened.
Conversation was simple.

"Let's go to the consignment shop."

"They went to the consignment shop."

"They'll be gone all day."

"Look what I got."

"It fits like a glove."

"Who's cooking?"

"Add cheese balls to the shopping list."

"Did you get the cheese balls?"

"How many cheese balls are left?"

"Do you want to go to the movies?"

"No."

"What are you going to do?"

"Probably nothing. Take a nap."

"You woke me up."

"If I can hear you, you are making too much noise."

"But she's never had an over-easy egg!"

"Who finished the puzzle?"

"Who ate the Cocoa Puffs?"

One memorable conversation among several meno-pausal and memory-challenged women covered a variety of topics without ever using a proper noun.

"You know the one I mean. The guy with all the tat-toos who used to date that woman who was in the movie about Vietnam."

"Was she blond?"

"I think so."

"I liked that movie."

In the early years we slept in tents on the wide yard over-looking miles of marshes with no other houses in sight. Having graduated from the tents, I now slept in the room called the nursery with Scarlet, Sage, any other women who straggled in during the week, and the occasional five-year-old who couldn't sleep with the other children. Af-ter all these years, Scarlet and Sage still couldn't believe that I wanted to talk before going to sleep, and I couldn't believe that they didn't. Nor did they read before going to sleep. They lay down, turned the lights out, closed their eyes, and went to sleep. I had known this for a long time, and I still found it incomprehensible. Possibly immoral. Over the years at Riverbend we had learned much about each other, who was calm and who worried, who snored, who got mad over Cocoa Puffs.

Privacy was nonexistent and order was out of the question. I kept my little cot neatly made, but otherwise there was no hope. By midweek the floors were exceptionally dirty. By the end of the week, the bottoms of my feet would be black.

Every year our week and a half at Riverbend was pretty much like every other. But in spite of its comforting sameness, this year was different. Most of our teenagers were now high school seniors. It was likely that this would be their last complete vacation at Riverbend. Next year they would have left for freshman orientation and we all, we mothers and fathers and friends, would feel different, and the loft would be quiet and it would be empty.

On Labor Day, we packed our cars, washed the floors, and put away the mattresses and bed frames. Summer was officially over.

We returned home to school and housework and the specter of college applications. University catalogs were requested and delivered and their slick marketing packages all began to look and sound the same. A few stood out. A few front-runners fell to the back of the pack. The information piled up a foot high. Soon each new arrival was casually tossed into a basket unread. Our denial was strong.

Scarlet and Sage, having had their children at a younger age, had already gone through this years before. But many of my friends were facing it for the first time. Our reactions varied from meditative surrender to my own attempt to maintain control by making several hundred lists. I made lists of colleges, lists of dates and deadlines, lists of phone calls, problems, and questions large and small. Harper made me stop when I began a list of the things she would have to bring with her when she *went* to college. I liked to think that I had only a little anxiety. I liked to think that, in marked contrast to a mere year before, I had no fear. That it was now time for this to happen, and that I did not feel like throwing up. But truth be told, now and then I *did* feel a little like throwing up, or weeping for a day or two, but I didn't. I began instead to organize my mind around the idea that she would go. I began to look at a photograph of her that sat on my bookcase, and tell her, *You can go. It is a good thing. I will be fine. You will be fine. All will be well.*

Tattoo Heaven

*L*ife resumed its ups and downs, its calls to firewood and mulch. I was, I confess, slightly disappointed that I had not, in my six weeks off, magically lost thirty pounds, just in case I decided at some point in the future to get a tattoo, or a knee replacement, or have sex. I'd foreseen a knee replacement ever since a ligament repair had come undone when I dropped several hundred pounds of drywall on my leg three days after moving into my house. I hoped to avoid the replacement, but just in case, I knew it would be easier if I were in shape. I wasn't so sure about the sex.

The tattoo was a new musing, certainly one I had not had in the days—was it only a year ago?—of the Catholic camp. Although I didn't want my daughter to have one— she was too young, I thought, to have an irreversible mark on her skin—I had come to admire them. I admired Angelina Jolie's and David Beckham's. (I really wasn't kidding about the 25 percent pop culture.) Getting a tattoo was something I occasionally thought about when trying to figure out how I could outwit (outsmart and outlast) age. And ever since *O, the Oprah Magazine* called me a suburban matron, I had been trying to figure out a way to prove it wrong.

Tattoo advice abounded. Don't get it where you can see it all the time; you'll get really tired of it. Don't get it on skin that is prone to wrinkling; the hands and wrists and neck are bad choices. Tattoos done over bone are unbelievably painful. The stories were discouraging. There was the woman who'd had a giant sunflower tattooed around her belly button. Then she got pregnant and that sunflower was never the same, and not in a good way. There was the Marine, Sage's cousin by marriage, who liked to show off his tattoo, rolling up the sleeve of his white T-shirt and pointing to a tiny blue dot on his biceps. *Hurt like hell,* he said. And then there were the multitudes who had had Chinese ideograms engraved upon themselves only to find out later that the words they thought had meant "mysterious" or "bravery" actually meant things like "weird" or "supermarket." I have a kimono jacket I love quite a lot—black with kanji symbols—but I always take it off before I go into a Japanese restaurant for fear that it says "Coca-Cola" or "Fuck you."

Before leaving for the summer, Harper had lobbied with a fierce intensity for me to let her get her septum pierced. For those of you fortunate enough not to know what that means, the septum is the small piece of flesh and cartilage between your nostrils. Pierced, it usually sports a ring. Think of the ring in a bull's nose. Although I had forbidden tattoos and body piercings (other than ears) while she still lived in my house and my permission was still legally required, I allowed her to show me about a hundred pictures of septum piercings she had found online. There was no getting around the fact that when you looked at someone with a septum piercing, you saw someone with a ring in the middle of his or her face, and although I knew that it was her moral right to do this to herself, and I wanted—in theory—to let her do it, I couldn't. She was, to put it mildly, stunned, and disappointed in my decision, in my lack of daring.

After her return, she resumed her lobbying, and for some godforsaken reason, I gave in. It was partly that I was tired of the pressure, partly that I thought she needed me to honor her desire. The day I said yes, we drove to a place called Tattoo Heaven in a small nearby city. On the way I pondered aloud that I might get a tattoo when we were there.

"What do you think?" I asked.

She—someone who had heard once too often about my imaginary lives—looked at me suspiciously. "For all I know," she said, "you already have one."

The large anteroom of Tattoo Heaven was dominated by a life-size plastic dragon well coated with dust. The only reason I didn't walk right back out was that the mother of one of Harper's friends had once day spent a pleasant hour chatting with Sully, the owner of the shop, while deciding whether or not to have him pierce her navel. This gave Sully a certain amount of credibility in my eyes, so, in spite of the dragon and my misgivings, we walked quickly to the counter and looked at the available nose jewelry. Then Sully walked in. Not what I expected. The rotund personification of serious body modification, Sully looked like a giant leprechaun caught in a staple factory, and although I decided not to judge him based on appearance, the sheer amount of metal strained my abilities.

Harper found the jewelry she wanted, and a young employee took it out of the open tray, the tray that God knows how many people had handled.

"Wait a minute," I said. "The jewelry isn't sterile?"

"We wipe it down with Betadine," he said.

"That isn't exactly sterile," said I. Sully stormed past the counter, scowling madly.

"It's how I've done it for twenty years, and I wrote the *book* on how to do tattoos," he said, his face glinting.

"That's comforting," I said.

Our second piercing parlor was several towns to the south. It was neat and clean and followed sterile procedures. There were no monsters in the waiting room and no plastic lizards. The piercer was a tall, excessively thin, and very sweet young man with green hair. Though he had only a few piercings, his lips were punctuated with miniature spears and throughout the entire nasal procedure I had to restrain myself from asking him how he kissed girls. The best I could figure was that some girls find making out with a boy with daggers in his lips quite dangerously exciting, and it was, I confess, an intriguing thought.

The piercing did not take long, looked like it hurt, and then was over. I thought it didn't look too bad. I thought she would get tired of it eventually, that Thomas would be furious, and that it would put the lobbying to rest. Thomas *was* furious, and the lobbying was over. The piercing lasted a week before it became infected and the ring had to be surgically removed.

As for me, it turned out that I wasn't ready for tattoos, or I was years *beyond* ready.

"Where would you get it?" Sage had once asked.

"Right shoulder."

"What would it say?"

"I can't tell you."

"Why not?"

I couldn't tell her because I didn't know. It changed

every day. It was alpha or omega or the sphinx, mysterious, hoarding secrets.

My body, I decided, was already covered with markings. The year of the black dog. The year of the boy named Shep. The year I became a mother, a wife, wrote a book, saw a meteor shower fill the sky for a week of dark nights. And I imagined future years: the year of my daughter's departure, the year of great sadness, the year of starting over. None random, none whimsical, none in kanji, none visible.

We think we are supposed to do the big thing, have the extreme moment, the moment when you leave your husband and run off with the postman, or smoke opium in Kuala Lumpur. But there's a difference between genuine experience and doing something just for the sake of doing it. It turns out that I thought daring was kind of overrated. I'd had daring. I'd already danced with the red dress on. I didn't need to prove anything, and I didn't need a tattoo.

Philosopher Kings:
A Windswept Mind

I thought all along that, eventually, Hunter and I would reunite. He was persistent and he was patient. I thought that sooner or later I would be worn down. I would meet him in the Berkshires or go to his hunting camp in New York where we would shoot arrows at hay bales and fish. Or he would pull unexpectedly in to my driveway in a battered light blue truck. But soon after Harper and I returned from Riverbend, it was Harold who called and asked if he could come to my house, with his son, one Sunday in October after competing in a minitriathlon in Six Mile Beach. I said yes, of course, but since he asked a month in advance, I had plenty of time to reconsider, to cancel, to become busy or have a personal emergency. I am not sure why—the extra pounds, the extra years—but I was nervous. The last time I had seen Harold, his son, Lucas, had been a round-faced baby trying to eat the leaves of a jade plant in my living room. Now he was twenty-three.

I was a poet when I knew Harold. The first time I met him he was eating a cucumber, whole and unpeeled, and said something vaguely provocative about it. Not sexual or offensive, but strange enough to pique my interest.

It was a good era. I lived in a tiny apartment in the attic of an old farmhouse I shared with a seventeen-year-old boy named Joe whose parents had left him there alone after they divorced and each remarried. Joe and I had a garden together. We rode on his motorcycle on dirt paths through the miles of woods surrounding the house. I wrote at a board desk in front of the window and once a microstorm or small tornado blew all the screens out of the house and every paper I owned onto the front yard.

Harold was sturdy and smart and unexpected. He was a good friend and a good lover. He was also a good cook, which made my subsequent failure to marry him incomprehensible to me now. In time he went to Africa with the Peace Corps and I went off to graduate school, where I met Hunter and had another life. But it was Harold who stood for the halcyon days of my early life as a poet. I was twenty-seven when I met him. Now, precisely one week after the nose ring removal, Harold sat at my kitchen table like a tired Buddha. Thirty years had passed.

Our children sat with us. Lucas was amiable and handsome. Harper was uncharacteristically quiet. Harold looked much the same as I remembered, strong and solid, black hair, though a little balder and flecked with gray. I felt, immediately upon seeing him, a comfortable energy. I remembered how much I had liked him and could tell right away that I liked him still. There was no awkward silence.

We ate pearl jelly and drank bubble tea that Harper had gotten at the Asian marketplace in the same nearby city that housed Tattoo Heaven. This was the kind of thing that you wouldn't do with everyone but was natural with Harold, who used to bake chicken with twenty heads of garlic. I had cookies, which I forgot to give them, and didn't have coffee, which they seemed to need. It was a cliché, I know, but it *was* as if no time had passed, except for the fact that our grown children sat there with us, and Harold was now a husband of twenty years. I knew his face and his tiredness and his dry humor. I felt at home with his mind, and it was a good feeling. The difference between e-mailing him and seeing him was the difference between hearing about bubble tea and tasting it.

Sitting across from him, at my big and scarred kitchen table, tired and in need of coffee, there was between us a sudden levity of years, his son, my daughter, the casual spark of our past together and the possibility of future friendship. I did not fully understand then why Harper's leaving was catapulting me not only into a future that often seemed full of peril, but also into the past, into memories of stones and fields, mothers and brothers, poets and hunters, the child, the youth, the mother, and whatever woman I was about to become.

Harper had asked me once, apropos of nothing in particular, if I was ever bored in Six Mile Beach, at our house, with my life, and I said no, not really. There was much work to be done or not done: gardening and sweeping and stacking firewood in neat rows with crisscrossed ends. There was the dog to walk, books to write, and furniture to move. But the truth was that although I told myself and everyone else that I was no longer a poet, and indeed had written only two poems in twenty years, and could barely stand to read poetry anymore, I missed the windswept mind that wrote it.

Harold was the ghost of an era long past. His presence in my kitchen reminded me that I might not need a boyfriend or a tattoo, but I needed Robert Hass and his painful radiance, and Mary Oliver—*It is easy to fall down on your knees when the shining rain begins to happen.* I needed Rumi: *I need more grace than I thought,* and Rilke with his scarred-faced and familiar angels. I needed poetry and poets and their promises of redemption. Theirs was a light I had missed and did not know how to recapture. I didn't want to be Picasso's lover, I discovered. I wanted to be Picasso. I wanted to be Rilke on the ramparts, taking dictation. I wanted to be Emily, listening.

The Ties That Bind

*M*aybe it was Harold and the pleasure of his company at my table, or maybe I just wanted to avoid driving to Connecticut, but as Thanksgiving neared, I suddenly wanted my family to be in my house, all of them at the same time. I went to them often. Now I wanted them to come to me. So when my mother said, "I think we need a change of scene this year," I said, "Come on up. We can have it here." Jack and Andrew said yes and before I knew it, I was committed. I had never cooked a turkey before or hosted a major holiday, but I was an organized person. How hard could it be? I thought.

Right away I was afraid of the turkey. It seemed to be what people talked about at Thanksgiving. The turkey was dry (said regretfully) or it was moist (said admiringly). As the day drew near, I ordered a turkey from a shop in town where people in the know ordered theirs. I had to decide how many pounds and was pretty sure I overestimated by about 100 percent. The turkey might be dry, but there would be a lot of it.

I bought a roasting pan. I bought a twelve-cup coffeemaker to augment the two-cup pot Harper had taken to Providence. I bought a tablecloth and napkins. I bought white hydrangeas from the boy in the flower shop. He wrapped them with pale purple and green organza ribbons, and, with a greed born in flower shops, I thought perhaps I would go back later for lilies, but I never did.

Instead, I went online and studied the recipes for a hundred "perfect Thanksgiving dinners." There were a bewildering number of ways to cook a turkey, all of them angling for the elusive moistness quotient. I quickly knew that I would not "loosen the skin and rub butter beneath the breast skin and put stuffing into the resulting pocket." Thomas, who was coming to the party, went online and looked up recipes with me over the phone at eleven o'clock the night before Thanksgiving.

"Here's a good one," he said, reading unhelpfully from a series of Thanksgiving disasters he had discovered online. "This guy leaves a note on his door saying, 'I fucked up the turkey and I've gone to the grocery store to get some real food.'"

"That's helpful," I said.

I finally decided to start the turkey breast side down. I had a complicated timetable. I had a meat thermometer. My old friend Morgan, from my Cambridge days, a stalwart and noble man recently separated from his wife, would bring four chairs to add to my own four. I was ready.

They came early. Jack showed up with his "babies"—six small ramekins of homemade crème brûlée—and a broken blowtorch. Andrew and Laura showed up with wine, cider, cheese and crackers, and a glorious array of olives. My mother showed up with two kinds of cranberry sauce (one with apricots and one with hot chili peppers), creamed onions, sweet potatoes, and squash pie.

"I can make the cranberry sauce," I had said.

"I have a recipe I want to try," she said.

"I can make the pie," I said.

"I have a recipe for a squash pie," she said. "I thought that might be fun instead of pumpkin." It was useless to even try talking her out of cooking, and I gave up. I would make the turkey and the stuffing, and she would make almost everything else. This was okay with me. I was not a good cook or a creative one, and once, in a fit of self-pity, I had cried on the living room couch that I was sorry I wasn't a good cook, and that I never knew what to make for dinner, and I was sorry we ordered out so much, and that Rose's mother was a better cook than I and that every time Harper went to her house she must regret not having a mother who cooked good food.

Harper had stood in the middle of the wide arched doorway and stared at me.

"I really don't care about it," she said. "I don't think about it at all." This made me feel a little better, but how could someone not want a mother who cooked? I wanted a boyfriend who could cook. If I met one, I knew, I would risk the werewolf.

In my family, the cooking gene has skipped a generation, and I am that generation. At family dinners, the appetizers alone send me into fits of low self-esteem. Baked Brie. Crab cakes. Home-baked pumpernickel bread stuffed with spinach dip. The desserts are just as daunting. Giant fruit tarts glazed with whatever fruit tarts are glazed with. Platters laden with several kinds of delicious homemade cookies made, to my amazement, by a single person.

Even Harper liked to cook. And not just cook, in my sense of the word, the basic sustenance kind of way, but blend, whisk, and fold. She could make piecrust. She could deglaze a pan. When we went to my mother's, they made pies, experimental desserts, dips, breads, main dishes, and sides of vegetables, all of which contained pints of cream, sticks of butter, vats of cream cheese, and liberal amounts of canned mushroom soup. For desserts, they added sugar to the mix, white, brown, or confectioners', take your pick. When they wanted to have a really good time they watched cooking shows. Once, when I was making dinner with them, Harper pulled the wooden spoon gently out of my hand and said, "Here. Let me do that."

And the origins of my cooking genes? When my brothers and I were children, we would watch in awe as our nineteen-year-old aunt ate half a watermelon or a quarter of a pie for breakfast. Her son told me not so long ago that when he visited her recently they had popcorn for dinner. Andrew ate peanut butter and jelly sandwiches for lunch every day for twenty years. After his divorce from my mother, my father ate every meal out for the rest of his life. His brother, my uncle, put ketchup on his mashed potatoes well into his adulthood. For all I knew, he still did.

In spite of my cooking challenges, my schedule went well. Because at my mother's house dinner is always two hours late, my goal was to have dinner at exactly the time I had said we would. I got a little upset when my mother, in careful accordance with the two-hours-late policy, resisted putting the onions and sweet potatoes in on time. I had to take a little bit of Rescue Remedy in a coffee cup.

"What's in that cup?" asked my mother, suspiciously.

"Diet Coke."

She said, "Are you sure?"

"Scotch," I said.

"That's not scotch," she said.

"Rum," I said.

"That's not rum," she said.

"Red wine," I said.

She shook her head. She knew I didn't drink, but seemed to think that this dinner might get me to hoist a glass or two.

In the end, everything went well, though Jack almost set the house on fire while torching the crème brûlée. But the table fit eight, the napkins were ironed, Morgan brought the chairs as planned, and the turkey was moist. The white hydrangeas were beautiful and radiant, and would remain so for weeks thereafter.

After dark, we went for a walk on the seawall. Jack and Morgan carried flashlights. I walked the dog. Small groups formed and broke up, conversations began and ended and resumed later in different configurations.

"Should I let her go to the dance?"

"I was shocked."

"This is what she said to me."

"Look at those birds. There are fish running." That was Andrew; it was the kind of thing he would notice.

Then we went home and sat or lay around in the living room peacefully, reading newspapers or dozing off in the leather recliners. Thomas fell asleep on the couch. Morgan told a joke. My mother knitted. Harper read. Jack went to bed.

Once, years ago, Jack and Andrew and I sat at my mother's kitchen table and talked with her about our childhood.

"Do you remember," I asked my mother, "when the sow would get loose from the Doanes' farm and they would call you so that you could get us inside before she got to our house?"

"I don't remember any sow," she said.

"There was a sow," said Andrew.

"There was?" asked Jack.

"And the orphan lamb we fed from a baby bottle?"

"I remember the lamb," said Jack. "That goddamn ewe charged me down."

"Remember when we rode Duncraggan?" I said.

"We did not ride that bull," said Andrew.

"I thought we did."

"No way."

"Okay, remember the time there was a rabid dog walking down the street and you got us in?" I asked my mother.

"I don't remember a rabid dog," said Andrew.

"There was a rabid dog," said my mother.

"Why don't I remember any of this?" asked Jack.

"You were too young," said Andrew.

"And Atticus came home and shot it," I said.

"Who was Atticus?" asked Jack, and I laughed. But there really was a sow, and a lamb, and there was a rabid dog, walking down the long dusty street, between the rows of sycamore trees with their dry and papery bark.

My mother could still recite the poems she learned by heart as a young child in the green hills of Connecticut where she walked to school under the watchful eyes of eagles. She could recite "I Wandered Lonely as a Cloud" and "Kubla Khan" in a lilting, chanting voice. This and other memories ran through my life like silver threads. I contemplated all that she had given us—will and art and a connection to the beauty of *place*—and I realized that in the face of her aging and Harper's leaving, what I was doing was checking all the lines, the ties, the bonds of our continuum, just to be sure that they would hold. Andrew and Jack and I were now the repositories of what my mother did and did not remember, and the memories of her mother and her mother's mother. And one day Harper would hold all of these memories and my own, and pass them to her children: the ten miles on horseback, and Rose in the boat, and the sow and the lamb and the great bull Duncraggan.

What Kind of Wind

Harper was accepted early to her first-choice college, and the eventuality of her leaving took yet another leap toward reality. She was smarter than I, and deeper, and wrestled with greater themes than I cared to now, having wrestled with them so long ago. She drove roads that I had not driven. We face new challenges when our children head out into the world. All of the small moments of letting go pale in the light of this larger one. And I knew there were even larger departures yet to come. But here we still were, safe in the same house for one more year. I planned to savor that year and ease gradually and gracefully into the next stage of our relationship. But sometimes when I hugged her, I refused to let go.

Much had happened in the past year. Harold and I continued to exchange e-mails. He sent me his writing, which I liked—both the writing itself and the fact that he sent it to me. Hunter sent me a "lucky wheat penny" for my birthday, and I put it on an off-white plate on a table beside my bed along with my earrings and my favorite reading glasses. I would meet him in the spring, in the hills of what now seemed like our childhood, but I didn't hold out a lot of hope for Hunter and me. Still, a door had been opened. I didn't know who I might love, Hunter, or some as yet undiscovered X, or the common eiders bobbing in the ocean like giant black and white corks, but I now was pretty sure I would love *someone*.

I began to envision other worlds, other lives, invisible cities, trying futures on for size. I began to imagine leaving Six Mile Beach. I *couldn't* imagine it, but the idea had been planted. I thought of going somewhere, visiting my imaginary dwelling places, meeting them like blind dates, listening to their stories of joy and failure, drinking their tea.

I didn't know what the future held in its mysterious and spacious arms. But I knew what I would take with me into that wilderness: the dread and angelic worlds living in the empty rooms of my heart, the shards of a green pot once smashed at the feet of a man with blue, blue eyes, leaf green light, a promise of wind. Houses and men and words and a haze of smoke that felt a lot like happiness. And maybe it *was* happiness. I didn't know if I could reclaim the independence or adventure of my youth, and I didn't know if I wanted to. But I knew I was ahead of the game. I had lived in interesting times. I had made shelters and protected them. I had given birth to a child I was proud to know. I was already a woman whose dreams had come true.

There is something that happens when you become a mother. You can hear your child's voice no matter what. In a roomful of children you hear her voice. From across a large distance, you can hear it. In the midst of great noise, you hear her.

One day that fall, Harper took her camera and went for a walk on the beach. In an hour or so she called me and asked if I would mind bringing her a new roll of film. She knew it was an imposition, and it was, and I did it anyway, because I wanted to.

The ocean was huge, the tide was near high, and fog had rolled in and cast its fine mist over everything. I found her, gave her the film, and we walked down onto the beach. Her hair was dark, her skin was fair, and her eyes were sea gray and a little wild. We both knew that my bringing the film didn't mean that I would be joining in on whatever adventure she was having, and we smiled and turned to walk in different directions. After a minute or two I heard her call me. I heard her over the thunder of the waves. I turned and saw her small in the distance, facing my way and waving. Even from far away, I could hear her. I could see that she was waving just to say thank you, just to say good-bye.

Years pass, and you return to your life as someone who doesn't live with a baby, a toddler, a child, a teenager. You return to your life as someone who doesn't tell someone else, with increasing futility, to get up in the morning, go to bed at night, and step away from the computer. You return to being a person strangely free of someone else's schedule: school hours, lessons, appointments. You return, but to what? Certainly not to the girl who sat in the poet-nun's office and contemplated her rakish love life.

Sometimes I think we don't change much at all. Hunter and Harold sounded just the way they always had, their syntax and extreme intelligence and quirky humor and language. Andrew's hair was gray and Jack's was receding, Harper would leave, and my mother would age, but we all still seemed to stand at the foot of the waterfall, young and immortal. It was as if twenty or thirty or fifty years had never passed, and I wondered if I, too, sounded the same, wrote the same, was the same. Harper and I used to play a game called Essences, in which one player thought of a person and the other asked questions and tried to guess who the person was. It had nothing to do with appearance or with the external vagaries of life, temporary fears or joys or sadness or daily woes. If this person were a tree, what kind of tree would it be? What kind of dog? What kind of chair? What kind of cheese? It took surprisingly little time to figure out who the person was. Hunter and Harold and Jack and Andrew made me wonder if the essence of a person ever really changed.

We get older and balder and wider and more wrinkled. We have our disappointments and our elations. The twin cyclones of marriage and parenthood hit and consume our souls. Careers happen. They fulfill or disappoint us. Days and days and days add to our noble faces and at the same time take away. Take away the newness of what we were, what our children now are, and maybe we have another chance to set forward into the promise of our future. Maybe everything unnecessary, everything false or fearful, is whittled away by time, and we *do* return to our essence, to whatever we have always been: what kind of tree, what kind of water, what kind of wind.

Acknowledgments

With heartfelt gratitude to:

Liv Blumer, agent and friend, for her patience, kindness, wisdom, and grace.

Danielle Friedman at Hudson Street Press, whose efforts made this a better book than it started out to be.

Luke Dempsey, editor in chief of Hudson Street Press.

The principal, administration, and teachers of the public high school in the town I call Six Mile Beach, for an impressive job under sometimes trying circumstances, and for doing well by all of its students, including my daughter.

Suzanne Cox, Marion Webster, Paula Duggins, Janet Brady, and Maureen Denney, for wisdom, support, and friendship.

Jack, for taking all of my phone calls; Andrew and Laura, for suspending disbelief; my mother, for being miraculous just the way she is; and Thomas, for being a great father and good friend.

Most of all for my daughter, all and everything, who is really so much cooler and more wonderful than I could ever convey.

About the Author

Catherine Goldhammer, author of the critically acclaimed *Still Life with Chickens* (Plume, May 2007), is a graduate of Goddard College and was a poetry fellow in the master of fine arts program at the University of Massachusetts in Amherst. Her poetry has been published in the *Georgia Review* and the *Ohio Review*. She lives in a small cottage on the coast of New England with her daughter, her dog, and a cat named Monkey.

B
GOLDHAMM
ER

Goldhammer,
Catherine.

Winging it.